JOURNALING AS A SPIRITUAL PRACTICE

Encountering God
Through Attentive Writing

HELEN CEPERO

IVP Books

An imprint of InterVarsity Press
Downers Grove, Illinois

RANCHO CUCAMONGA
PUBLIC LIBRARY

Special thanks to Mandy Bankson
for her loving friendship and trustworthy reading.

InterVarsity Press

P.O. Box 1400, Downers Grove, IL 60515-1426

World Wide Web: www.ivpress.com

E-mail: email@ivpress.com

©2008 by Helen Cepero

All rights reserved. No part of this book may be reproduced in any form without written permission from InterVarsity Press.

InterVarsity Press® is the book-publishing division of InterVarsity Christian Fellowship/USA®, a student movement active on campus at hundreds of universities, colleges and schools of nursing in the United States of America, and a member movement of the International Fellowship of Evangelical Students. For information about local and regional activities, write Public Relations Dept., InterVarsity Christian Fellowship/USA, 6400 Schroeder Rd., P.O. Box 7895, Madison, WI 53707-7895, or visit the IVCF website at <www.intervarsity.org>.

Scripture quotations, unless otherwise noted, are from the New Revised Standard Version of the Bible, copyright 1989 by the Division of Christian Education of the National Council of the Churches of Christ in the USA. Used by permission. All rights reserved.

The excerpt from "Le Cri de Merlin" on p. 132 is from Burning World by Robert Collen (Althol, Mass.: Haleys, 1997). Reprinted with permission.

Every effort has been made to trace and contact copyright holders for materials quoted in this book. The author will be pleased to rectify any omissions in future editions if notified by the copyright holders.

Design: Cindy Kiple

Images: John Rawsterne/iStockphoto

ISBN 978-0-8308-3519-5

Printed in the United States of America ∞

g green press *InterVarsity Press is committed to protecting the environment and to the responsible use of natural resources. As a member of Green Press Initiative we use recycled paper whenever possible. To learn more about the Green Press Initiative, visit <www.greenpressinitiative.org>.*

Library of Congress Cataloging-in-Publication Data

Cepero, Helen, 1951-

Journaling as a spiritual practice: encountering God through attentive writing / Helen Cepero.

   p. cm.

Includes bibliographical references,

ISBN 978-0-8308-3519-5 (pbk.: alk. paper)

1. Spiritual journals—Authorship. 2. Spiritual life—Christianity.

I. Title.

BV4509.5.C4235 2008

248.4'6—dc22

2008008907

P	25	24	23	22	21	20	19	18	17	16	15	14	13	12	11	10	9	8	7	6	5	4	3	2	1
Y	29	28	27	26	25	24	23	22	21	20	19	18	17	16	15	14	13	12	11	10	09	08			

CONTENTS

INTRODUCTION

><

My husband and I traveled to the tropical islands of Samoa for our twenty-fifth wedding anniversary. Before we left, both of us thought we knew why we chose to travel so far away from our home in Chicago. For my husband, who loves planning trips, Samoa was uncharted territory for exploration and discovery. For me, visiting the Samoan islands was an opportunity to be in a relatively unspoiled tropical setting and walk along pristine beaches next to turquoise water. For both of us, it was a time to celebrate the life that we have together.

Walking along the white sandy beach on the island of Ofu in American Samoa, I did find myself gazing out at a clear turquoise sea. But if that was all I did, I would have missed the best of Samoa. Beautiful as the landscape was, an even greater beauty lay beyond the sand, underneath the ocean's surface. When I share pictures of our visit to Samoa, I point to the shadowed area on the clear water and express my regret that we did not bring an underwater camera, because I spent most of our ten days on Ofu wearing a snorkeling mask and fins, looking at some of the most varied coral reef in the world and swimming with fish of indescribable variety and color.

These pages are also the beginning of a journey, one that you have chosen for reasons at least as varied as any other trip you have taken in your life. Some of you are longtime journal keepers who wonder what could be added to a practice already so firmly established in your lives. Others of you might have tried to keep a journal at times in the past but never really kept it up as a regular practice. Perhaps some of you have never kept a journal at all. It does not matter where you are in your journaling experience. What does matter is your desire and willingness and commitment to honor this spiritual practice by intentionally going below the surface. It is here that God wants to surprise you with the beauty of your own life, growing and alive, filled with movement, light and shadow. It is here that God wants to meet your own longing for a deeper life with the Spirit's even greater longing to be with you, in all of who you were and are and will be. The journaling practices presented in this book are simply the mask, the snorkel and the fins that will allow you to make this journey. You will carry your own underwater camera—the journal itself—recording all that you see and hear, know and understand.

Every chapter of this book gives you opportunities along the way to use your journal reflections as a way of bringing your own life and world into sharper focus. Using your journal as a camera lens will allow you to zoom up close on a particular aspect of your own journey or take a step back and see the bigger picture of what might be going on within you and around you. These opportunities for seeing and remembering and recording are woven into the text of this book, just as they are woven into the text of your own life. If you do not actually stop to journal, you will only stay on the surface of my words and may not capture the greater beauty that is there right now in the context of your life. But if you stop as you read and take some time to follow the journaling suggestions along the way, you will meet your own exploring self beneath the text of this book as well as the God who longs to be with you on your journey.

Sometimes we might choose to explore with our journal as our only traveling companion. But there are other seasons in our life when we are helped in our own journey by having times and places to share the trip with others. A regularly meeting journaling group, even if it is only two or three people, can keep each person accountable and provide a group context for prayer and celebration. At the end of this book is an appendix with suggested guidelines to make the journaling group a safe place to write and reflect together. Especially in the beginning, it will be important to discuss the whole process of journaling, using questions such as, "How did that go for you?" or "What did you find helpful for staying with your journaling practice, and what made it difficult for you to keep writing?" As you become comfortable, try writing during the group's meeting time as well. Being in the presence of others, reflecting and writing together on the same journaling suggestion, can push us to go to a deeper, truer place within ourselves and with God.

The more authentically we travel into our own lives and our own stories, the more we will lay claim to God's image deep within us. This is both the beginning point and the destination. The more deeply we immerse ourselves in the story of God, the more our lives are filled with the love of Christ. This is my hope for all of you who read and write from these pages. And the more available we are to God, the more available we are to truly love ourselves, one another and the world. This is my prayer for all of you who make this journey, that through your reading and especially your journal writing you might "comprehend, with all the saints, what is the breadth and length and height and depth, and to know the love of Christ that surpasses knowledge, so that you may be filled with all the fullness of God" (Ephesians 3:18-19).

So we begin with a blessing for the journey ahead and below and above and in us:

In the name of the God who creates us, may we deepen our awareness of God's presence.

In the name of Jesus Christ, who goes before us, may we be led into pathways of truth.

In the name of the Holy Spirit, who is power and breath, may we sense the Spirit's movement in our lives.

May your journal be your companion and friend, your guide and counselor, through "him who by the power at work within us is able to accomplish abundantly far more than all we can ask or imagine" (Ephesians 3:20).

1

STARTING OUT

Discovering a Journaling Practice

>━━━━━━<

Fourth grade was the "California year" for each of my three children, who attended elementary school in northern California. This meant spending that particular year learning about all things California, especially California history. They studied the Ohlone Indians, the native tribe of the Bay Area; the Spanish priests who built missions along the Pacific coastline; and the miners who made their fortunes in the 1849 gold rush. As part of the year's study, the children went on a field trip with their class to pan for gold in the foothills of the Sierra Mountains. After a long bus ride, the fourth graders eagerly scrambled up the mountainside to the stream to begin their hunt for gold. Using a small sifter, each child dug into the stream, sifting through the river mud and rocks, searching for telltale flecks of gold. Sometimes the children would get discouraged; they would turn to their teacher and insist that there was no gold there after all. But inevitably one or two persistent students who kept digging and sifting patiently would find the flecks and even the tiny nuggets of gold that can still be found in the foothills of the Sierras. It didn't take long before the rest of the children saw what their classmates found and went back to enthusiastically dipping their own sifters in the stream's icy water.

Your journal is like the sifter my children used to pan for gold. If you are willing to dip your journal into the stream of your life, even though it may mean getting a bit wet and muddy, you will find the gold of your own life and God's eternal presence. One of the wonders of journaling is that it interprets us to ourselves. Here we find our own lives and discover that even the struggles we face are shot through with the gold of God's presence. But this blessing will not be ours unless we actually take up our journals and begin the process of sifting through our life experiences. It can be seductively interesting for us to read about journaling but not actually put our pen to paper or our hands to the keyboard. There is risk in the writing, but that is also where the reward is found. Buried in the stuff of our lives, underneath the running current of daily activities, lies the treasure, if only we are willing to risk looking and seeking.

When we go below the surface of our life's stream, we know from our own experience that this sense of God is not just past history or a lovely metaphor; it is a reality to be felt and touched, tasted and heard, perhaps even smelled. All spiritual disciplines and practices, including journaling, are about learning to be aware and awake, open to God, ourselves and the world around us. Journaling is meant to give clarity to your day and rest to your night, reminding you even when you are not writing in your journal that God is there with you, in and through it all.

Our true goal is a deeper relationship with the God who longs to meet us at the heart of all that we were and are and hope to be. Attention to our own reality—our dreams and our wounds, our desires and our hopes, our friends and our enemies, our past, our present and our future—is not for its own sake, but to tune our hearts to hear God's transforming Word for us. Our journal writing begins with our willingness to let God accompany us from the very beginning as we dip our journal-sifters into the running streams of our own lives.

⤳ *Beginning with God*

Before we take up our journals and pay attention to our lives, we begin with our willingness to be known utterly and completely by God. Make this prayer from Psalm 139 your daily prayer as you prepare to take up your journal and begin sifting through your own life:

O God! Dig into my life and know me heart to heart.
Test, probe, purify me! And pierce through
  my thoughts—
See whether I be on a road headed for grief,
And take me by the hand instead on the way of everlast-
ing life. (Psalm 139:23-24)

Praying this prayer makes clear our intention to invite God into the heart of all our practice even before we open our journals.

When I begin a walking or running exercise routine, I may well turn to friends who are experienced in it to recommend a brand of walking or running shoe. But these friends never recommend that I run in their shoes. They know that the shoes I will wear need to be fitted to my own particular feet; they must be exactly my size. And even if I wear the same size shoe, I cannot exercise in someone else's running shoes. Athletic shoes conform to the original wearer's own feet, and secondhand use gives support in all the wrong places, resulting in painful blisters.

A spiritual practice such as journaling might be started in response to a recommendation by a friend or colleague. But unless we find a practice that fits our life and the way we are created, it may give us more pain than joy. It is essential to begin by finding a journaling practice that fits who we are and where we are right now. Our beginning point is always the place where we are standing (or much more likely, sitting) right now. Though we walk along the way together with our friends and our family, our neighbors and our faith communities, we do not all walk in the same way. Each of us has peculiarities and gifts that we bring to journal keeping, and these need to be respected and honored.

Take a few moments now to reflect on how the practice of journaling might fit in your day or week, in your family life and in your devotional practice. In order to honor this activity, consider carefully when would be the best time for you to write.

⟫⟫ FINDING A TIME ⟪⟪

Look back over the past week, or even longer, and ask yourself these questions: Am I a morning person, or do I really understand and think better in the evenings? Is there a time in the middle of my day when the children are quiet or the office buzz is stilled, giving me a few moments for reflection? If it seems especially difficult to find an available time, invite God to help you see a place in your schedule that might be missing from your own vision.

When we journal as a spiritual practice we begin with an openness toward God's movement in our life and a desire to follow Jesus Christ. Such an intention makes journal writing prayerful writing.

There is not just one "right" time for prayer, and the time of our daily or weekly prayer might change in different seasons of our lives. As a mother of three small children, I found that setting aside an extended time once a week was more possible than trying to carve out even a few moments from my busy days. In monastic settings, morning and evening, noonday and nighttime were all times that Christians would meet for prayer. If this is an unfamiliar practice, begin with short times of five or ten minutes each. It is better to make even a small start than not to journal at all because the ideal time is not available to you.

Just as there is no right amount of time to devote to journal keeping, there is also no right place. A coffeehouse can be just as appropriate as a prayer room in a church or retreat house. But all spiritual practices benefit from returning again and again to the comfort of a familiar place and time. We honor our journal keeping by writing in a place that attracts us and that is also somewhere we can feel at home in ourselves.

FINDING A PLACE

Is it easy for you to listen when you are in a coffeehouse surrounded by other people, or do you need to be alone in a quiet room? Is there a room or nook in your home for journaling, or will you need to claim a space at your workplace? Will you sit at the kitchen table near a window in the morning light or in a comfortable chair at the end of the day when the children are in bed? Perhaps you will want to take a few quiet moments at your office desk and put the incoming calls on hold.

Sometimes just a few small changes can reveal a space available for reflection. A friend complained that she could not find a space in her home for prayer. Everything around her seemed only to remind her of what she still needed to accomplish before the day's end. But as she sat in her living room, she saw the large tree in her backyard. By turning the living-room chair just ninety degrees, she was able to make this beautiful tree an anchor for her prayer time and journal keeping, and so she found rest for her soul. Some of us find a place at home or at work, but others will need to look around for a third place. A coffeehouse was my personal sanctuary for the season of my life when my home was filled with the happy but distractingly noisy demands of children. You might consider using a corner in the library, an Internet café or the empty room after your yoga class has ended.

For some of you, ensuring the privacy of your journal in your home will be very important. Having privacy gives you permission to write whatever comes to you; it allows you to make the journal wholly yours. Along the way you may choose to share something from your journal as a way of sharing yourself with a loved one. But some of us feel the approval or disapproval of those around us more intensely than the hopes and dreams of our own hearts. Worse yet, some of us have been violated by others who did not respect or love those hopes and dreams. We will never truly begin until we begin with the permission to say what must be said, to feel what must be felt and to be as honest as we are able to be for the sake of our own souls.

Choose a place to keep your journal that will ensure, as much as you are able, that its privacy will be respected. Even when writing with others, only you have the right to share from your own journal. If you are using the computer, think of a way of informing others that your journal is not to be read. Even within my own "Helen" file folder on the family computer, I have another file that is personal and private.

➤ CHOOSING A JOURNAL ➤

The stores are full of blank journals with many different kinds of bindings and covers. Will you begin with a new journal or pick up where you left off last year or yesterday? One workshop teacher suggested that it is best to use loose-leaf paper and a three-ring binder with dividers. That way you can have different sections for different types of journaling. Another author always has at least two journals—a larger one at home and a smaller notebook to carry with her. My daughter keeps three journals: a tiny journal that fits inside her purse and often has lists of reminders, a larger journal for reflections, and a travel journal that can easily be packed for trips away from home.

I especially like to write in the bound composition book with the mottled black-and-white cover. The lines are wide enough to accommodate my script when I write fast, and the books are cheap enough that I don't need to worry about writing too much. These books also lie flat for writing, an important criterion for me. Some of you who might want to draw or sketch in your journal should consider choosing an unlined book. Anyone who hopes to write outside the lines— literally or figuratively—might also choose an unlined journal or an artist's sketchpad.

Choosing a journal can be an important beginning to finding a journaling practice that belongs to you and fits the particular way God made you. It is also the beginning of honoring a spiritual practice and ultimately honoring your relationship with God and with yourself. Some of you will choose not to write in a book at all but will use your computer to both write and store your journal. Try making even the computer file a set-apart place by giving your e-journal its own file location, title and special font.

Take some care to select a journal that expresses who you are as well as a pen that will always be there when you want to write. If you are journaling on your computer, take some time there as well to set up your journaling practice. Making your time and place less haphaz-

ard clarifies your intention to follow through on your desire to keep
a journal. Being intentional also helps you pay attention during the
actual journal-writing time.

WRITING IN YOUR JOURNAL

Whatever choice of pen or paper you make, do not let your tools be
so precious that you cannot use them with abandon. One of the most
important rules of journaling is that you need to be free to write the
worst junk in the entire world. Most of us need to write ourselves
into a place of understanding. If we feel the need to be meaningful
right at the start, it can give us a severe case of writer's block. For
those of you who feel you can't write because of the memory of
a teacher's red marks on a paper where you shared what was true
and real for you at a moment in your childhood, this is especially
important.

Allowing yourself to write without regard to sentence structure,
spelling mistakes, paragraphs, finding the right word or even making sense gives you the permission and the freedom to come home to
yourself and God in your writing. Give yourself lots of space to say or
draw or imagine whatever asks to be heard, and keep your own red
pen locked in a drawer or hidden somewhere. Better still, throw it in
the garbage.

Writing your first thoughts without any internal or external re-
visions, or just trying to write without stopping for ten to twenty
minutes, will help to free up the flow between your head and your
pen on the paper or your fingers on the keyboard. Like the stretch-
ing exercises that one might do before running or swimming, "flow
writing" is a good way to warm up before beginning a journaling
exercise.

✐ WRITING YOUR FIRST THOUGHTS ✐

Begin with a time of silence or music or even physical exercise such as walking. Then simply put your pen in your hand and begin writing. It doesn't have to make sense, and you don't have to write in sentences or even sensibly. You can make lists or complain about journaling, but you must keep writing for ten minutes without stopping, even if it means repeating the same word over and over. If you feel stuck, try writing with your nondominant hand and see what happens. Or begin with the words "I remember," and write for five minutes. Then turn to a new page and begin with the words "I don't remember"; again write for five minutes. Here are the rules: Keep your hand moving, and don't cross out mistakes or worry about punctuation or grammar. Lose control and don't think or be logical. If something comes out that seems scary or exposed, dive right in because it probably has a lot of energy.

Always put the date at the top of each journal entry. This may seem unnecessary at first, but it will prove important if you want to go back and remember not only the entry itself but its surrounding events. Sometimes the time of day and the place also matter for a journal entry, so don't hesitate to record those. What we write in a hospital waiting room late at night differs from what we write in a coffee shop after a long, satisfying walk. The intention of a journal is to record and save the moment. It also offers the possibility of returning and reconnecting at a future time.

When we journal, we find that there is something about putting pen to paper (or fingers to the keyboard) and simply writing that seems to clear away the debris so that we can more clearly discern our lives and the world around us. But journaling as a spiritual practice means that we begin with the longing to come closer to God through our journaling. Like all spiritual practices, it begins with the trust that God is active at the heart of our lives and the life of the world. It begins with our openness to trusting in the transforming power of Christ's Spirit to lead us closer to our true selves and to God. As we regularly and intentionally pray in this way, we discover that "God is already present in the hidden depths of the present moment; it is just because we were skimming along across the surface of what is happening that we were unable to know and rest in that presence."

2

BEGINNING . . . AGAIN

Staying in My True Calling

>๛๛<

Trosly, France; Tuesday, August 13, 1985
This is the first day of my new life! Though it sounds melodramatic, I cannot avoid feeling that something significant is starting today. My decision to leave Harvard Divinity School and move to France to live for at least a year with Jean Vanier and his L'Arche community in Trosly took many tears and sleepless nights. It came after a period of many hesitations and inner debates. But as I drove away . . . I felt as if I were moving toward a new freedom.

The Road to Daybreak is a candid and intimate reflection on Henri Nouwen's life in the L'Arche community in France and at Daybreak in Canada. It is one of several journals Henri Nouwen wrote at key turning points in his life. Shining through all of Nouwen's journals is his willingness to risk new experiences in his search for an intimate relationship with God. Reading these journals, one doesn't doubt his strong sense of belonging to God, but he is transparent about his own faith struggles as well.

Friday, December 13

Yesterday was not only the day on which Peter left, but also the day on which I received a long letter from Daybreak in Canada inviting me to join their community. . . . I know Joe's invitation is not a job offer but a genuine call to come and live with the poor. They have no money to offer, no attractive living quarters, no prestige. This is a completely new thing. It is a concrete call to follow Christ, to leave the world of success, accomplishments, and honor, and to trust Jesus and him alone. . . . If ever I wanted a concrete sign of Jesus' will for me, this is it. I feel many hesitations. Living with handicapped people in a new country is not immediately attractive.

The questions raised in Nouwen's journals are more than self-examination; they are the seeds that plant renewal and transformation in his life. Nouwen has the space to move from utter certainty to naming all the hesitations and questions in his soul within a sentence or two, and only then does he find the place where he is called to "trust Jesus and him alone"—only to admit again to doubts about this particular call.

Like Nouwen, I am often sure of something yet unsure at the same time. I want and I do not want; I am attracted and repelled. I may long to move in a certain direction, but my resistance to going in that direction feels equally strong. I want to get it right and have my uncertainties sorted out and the truth understood. But if I would not write in my journal until I understood everything clearly, I might never begin at all. It is the writing itself that leads me into understanding.

Like me, some of you might have a collection of half-completed journals that were bought with the best of intentions or received with love from friends or family. I began these journals with the firmest resolve because the urge to write in order to understand myself and God felt "right" at the time. But the journal writing never really became a practice; it never grew into journal keeping. When I run across one of those journals, I feel a sense of guilt. Unfortunately, in journal writing as in nearly all spiritual practices, such a sense of guilt is not a very effective long-term motivator for developing habits of reflection and prayer. Beginning with a sense of failure often means that even with a firm resolve, a journal can end up gathering dust on the bookshelf.

In the journals of Henri Nouwen, it is clear that it is not his human resolve or personal effort that motivates him to keep writing in his journal. It is his overwhelming longing to be with God in all that he does and says, in all of who he is and hopes to be. When Nouwen is honest and true about his mixed feelings and motives, he finds God's hospitable welcome to all of who he is. This is what keeps him writing through his fears and his doubts toward new understandings and a sense of hope.

Without the kind of loving acceptance that Nouwen found in his journal, it would be difficult to continue in a journal-keeping practice. If you feel guilty about not writing but reluctant to continue, you are not alone. But rather than redoubling your journaling effort, place your hands on your journal and pray for greater, more loving and infinitely more capable hands to enfold your journal and your hopes of keeping a journal.

One of the constant invitations of Scripture is to return. "Return to the LORD, your God, for he is gracious and merciful, slow to anger, and abounding in steadfast love" (Joel 2:13). Returning is not always easy, as the prophet himself admits, but those who return will always find a welcome with God. If we had not begun at all, then it would not be possible to return again and again. We cannot continue in a practice never truly begun.

Let your journal be a place of returning, of clarification and finally of the grace of discovering that God is indeed compassionate and loving. Begin today with what we both know at the depth of your own heart is true—that you have the strong desire to meet God in your life and in your world. This desire will only grow as you remain in it because it is also in the depth of God's heart. Your own longing and God's desire for you are the motivating forces that will continue to bring pen to paper or return you to the keyboard.

Paraphrasing a Psalm

Read aloud these verses from Psalm 42, and sense the deep longing of the psalmist:

As a deer longs for flowing streams,
   so my soul longs for you, O God.
My soul thirsts for God,
   for the living God.
When shall I come and behold
   the face of God? (Psalm 42:1-2)

Now pause and see if you can think of a simile that captures your own longing or desire or hope. For example, just as my child lies in bed and listens to me read him a story, so I long to hear God's own story unfold in my life. Or just as an exhausted worker comes home after putting in a full day, takes off her shoes and rests on the couch, so I long to be able to simply rest in God. Or just as a shrub is planted in the ground, its roots reaching for water and its leaves toward the sun, so I long to be rooted in God's Word and bathed in God's loving light. Or just as a train follows the track and finds its destination, so I long to be able to stay on track and sense the Lord leading me in my decisions about where I am headed. How would you describe the longing and desire of your own heart using such a word picture?

Fear can also be a barrier to staying with a journaling practice. We fear that our own deep fears and anxieties will be exposed and our own inadequacies will become painfully obvious. We fear that if we recognize our hurts and wounds, they might overwhelm us. And we fear that in moving closer to God, we will lose ourselves, or at least our illusions about who we are. But what if it is at the heart of our deepest fears and most obsessive anxieties that God most wants to meet us?

Anne Lamott, a recovering alcoholic and a new single mother of an infant, writes about her fears in her journal *Operating Instructions: A Journal of My Son's First Year*. While she may have been an anxious mother at times, she is a bold and fearless journaler.

October 23

Half the time I'm completely winging this motherhood business. . . . Sam was so exasperating that I could feel fury coursing through my system, up my arms into my hands, like charged blood. I made myself leave the room, just left him crying in his bassinet in the living room, which is what Bill Rankin said to do once before. I went to the tiny bedroom in the back, and breathed and prayed for major help. The next thing I knew, I had decided to take him for a walk in the stroller in the dark. It was warm and the stars were just coming out; the sky seemed unusually deep. I said to God, I really need help tonight, I need you to pull a rabbit out of a hat.

Lamott's journal gives a sense of community and comfort to mothers—and not just to first-time or single mothers—who feel that they are "completely winging" motherhood but have no place to admit their sense of inadequacy. In her journal pages, she names not only her own inadequacies but also her need for God. Passionate about God and about her son, Anne Lamott is at times frightened and grateful, filled with sadness and overflowing with joy. As her words pour out on the page, it is not pretty or even pious in any way that we might understand. Instead it is mostly raw and real and feels undeniably true. And it all can get said in the safest of all places, her personal journal.

November 30

It is so hard to keep my sticky little fingers off the controls of this spaceship, especially when I get scared, like now when God has not bothered to give me the specific details of his solution to our financial needs. I'm just a little edgy being in the dark about it. . . . I would prefer he be more like Jeeves, streaming into rooms like sunlight with all that I need to feel comfortable—God as cosmic butler. The other way is so hard. . . . I have a deep belief that I know what is best for me and, now, by extension, what is best for Sam. The fact that I have spent my life proving that just the opposite is true does not keep me from acting like a schizophrenic traffic cop with a mission and a bullhorn.

Sometimes the fear itself is overwhelmed by the love that fills a mother's heart, and even Lamott sees the way that love can heal her and lead her closer to God.

March 20

Maybe if I can learn to breathe and go slower, I can somehow help Sam be spared some of the craziness I had in my life, all that chasing down of these things that I thought would make me okay or would prove that I was okay. A lot of it, looking back was metaphorically the serpent in the garden. . . . Still, you know what the name Samuel means? It means "God has heard." Like God heard me, heard my heart, and gave me the one thing that's ever worked in my entire life, someone to love.

Lamott tells the story of a two-year-old who gets locked inside a room with his mother on the other side of the locked door. The only thing the mother could do was slip her fingers under the door and hold on to her son's fingers in the dark until he stopped crying. Lamott writes,

June 16

I keep thinking of that story, how much it feels like I'm the two-year-old in the dark and God is the mother and I don't speak the language. She could break down the door if that struck her as being the best way, and ride off with me on her charger. But instead, via my friends and my church and my shabby faith, I can just hold onto her fingers underneath the door. It isn't enough, and it is.

Through her journal, Lamott is able to hold on to God. Your journal is also a way to hold on to God during times when life feels slippery and out of control. Or when you realize that the control you had so carefully planned out is an illusion.

➤ Write a Letter to God

If we think of psalms as letters to God, it is easy to see that the psalmists wrote letters of praise and joy but also of worry and sadness, lament and anger—and sometimes all in the same psalm! Tell God where you are in your story; tell God where you wish you were. Tell God how you see

yourself and how you see God. But be truthful rather than
nice. Be honest rather than the way you think you ought
to be.

Sometimes we are reluctant to journal because we are unwilling to
believe that the pursuit of self-understanding matters at all. A journal
begun with enthusiasm at a workshop or retreat now languishes because in our "real" world, it seems to be an indulgence. Maybe we hear
an inner voice persistently ask, "Why should I feel I have anything of
interest to say? Isn't this time spent journaling just contributing to the
narcissistic, selfish culture around me? Or why would anyone, least of
all me, want to remember what it was that I wrote about during a difficult time in my life?" Some think journaling is about autobiography,
or even the show-and-tell that we so often see on television talk shows
like Oprah's.

But as a spiritual practice, journaling is really about authenticity,
not exposing ourselves. Finding our unique self and personal call is
at the heart of understanding our identity and purpose as Christians.
Like the treasure hidden in a field, or the pearl of great price, this is
the discovery born not out of what we know or have but out of our
awareness of who we are and whose we are. As John Calvin insisted,
"There is no deep knowledge of God without a deep knowledge of self
and no deep knowing of self without a deep knowing of God."

Consider the Quakers, whose early diaries were written as a way to
accomplish self-examination, gratitude and ultimately self-transcendence.
One of the most famous of these journal keepers was John Woolman,
a Quaker who lived from 1720 to 1777. Woolman wrote a remarkable
diary about his conversion to faith and his personal vision of God. In
1757, Woolman was already struggling with the "Negro question" by
refusing to write wills when slaves were part of the property to be

inherited. But he writes in his journal that after waking up from a short sleep, he saw a light in his bedroom that he described as a "clear, easy brightness and near the center the most radiant." Then "words were spoken to my inward ear which filled my whole inward man . . . the language of the Holy One spoken in my mind. The words were, 'Certain Evidence of Divine Truth.'" His deep faith convicted him that the inner light that he as a Quaker saw in every person was also found in Negro slaves.

This realization led him on a journey to the southern colonies, where he visited every Quaker plantation owner who was also a slave-holder—and there were many. In his journal, Woolman recounts sitting down with each slaveholder, explaining carefully and thoughtfully what he believed, and convincing them that slavery was antithetical to the teachings of the Bible and Quaker faith. By the time of his death, there were no Quaker slaveholders left in the South. Much later, the Quakers were staunch abolitionists, and their homes were stations in the Underground Railroad. But it was John Woolman's journal, which reflected on the significance and meaning of his beliefs and his faith, that began this remarkable movement of emancipation of slaves owned by southern Quakers.

﹏ Witnessing to the Truth

> List those places or situations in your own life or in the world around you where you see, as Woolman did, "Certain Evidence of Divine Truth." Where are you being asked to speak out and name a wrong being done to you or someone you know? Where are you being called to bring light to a situation that has been dimmed by the darkness of misunderstanding or sin? Where might you need to change

everyday habits that make the environment within you
and around you worse? Where does the truth need to be
named and lived?

Doubt, fear, faith struggles and feelings of insignificance can all
cripple our journaling practice if they stay locked within us. But if
we allow all of this to flow out of us and onto the page, we just might
find our way through to a life lived with God, as well as a new sense
of self-knowledge. If we wait until we can get our faith lives "right" or
make sure our motivations are unmixed or keep our minds and hearts
clear, we will never begin a true spiritual practice at all. The journal
is a starting place for dealing with all the faith struggles that are still
going on, the doubts that linger and the fears that lurk. Saying them
"aloud" on the page helps us find the courage to continue, courage
that is rooted not in our personal effort but in God's eternal love for
each of us.

3

LOOKING INTENTLY

Paying Attention to My Life

>━━ ━━<

It doesn't have to be
the blue iris, it could be
weeds in a vacant lot, or a few
small stones; just
pay attention, then patch

a few words together and don't try
to make them elaborate, this isn't
a contest but the doorway

into thanks, and a silence in which
another voice may speak.
MARY OLIVER, "PRAYING"

The primary wonder of our Christian faith is that God comes to the place where we are and says our name. This is the nature of our God, who begins the biblical story by walking with Adam and Eve in the Garden of Eden. And even after there is separation between them, God pursues them with the poignant question, "Where are you?" It is a question that echoes throughout the Old Testament and then reverberates again and again in the New Testament. Surely God knows where we are, even when we are lost or unaccounted for in some other way. So the question is not some sort of celestial attempt to determine our location. Instead it seems to arise out of the longing of God's own heart that we would be aware and awake both to where we are and to God's presence in the place where we are. It is a question that invites us to be alert to God's presence and alive to God's love, wherever we are. As the psalmist insists,

If I ascend to heaven, you are there;
    if I make my bed in Sheol, you are there.
If I take the wings of the morning
    and settle at the farthest limits of the sea,
even there your hand shall lead me,
    and your right hand shall hold me fast.
If I say, "Surely the darkness shall cover me,
    and the light around me become night,"
even the darkness is not dark to you;
    the night is as bright as the day,
    for darkness is as light to you. (Psalm 139:8-12)

One of the best gifts of a journal is that it gives you a place to show up. As you write, you may discover where you actually are. When you know where you are, you may also see what is true, hear your own voice, gain an understanding of something that has troubled or puzzled you or savor again a joy that might have slid right by you almost unnoticed. Most of all, you will gain a clearer view of God's presence with you, in you and around you. Your journal is a place to celebrate the concrete details of yourself, your family, your community and the world. Noticing it all—every living, breathing detail that you are able to—is the spiritual work of your journal.

➤ Naming What I See—or Not

Spend a few minutes looking carefully around you at the

place where you are reading and writing just now. Ask yourself, *What do I see?* Perhaps there is a window, photos, a book you are reading or a lamp that you bought at an antique store. Write about what you see for another five minutes without stopping to correct or reflect on your writing. Then turn the page and ask yourself, *What do I not see?* Write for another five minutes without stopping to correct or reflect on your writing. Then reread both of these journal entries and write a response to what you saw and what you did not see.

Sometimes writing in a journal for even twenty minutes can seem like too long for people with busy lives filled with necessary obligations. Staying with the writing, however, can often prove fruitful, even if nothing seems to be happening. When we take a long look, we may see something that we would have missed if we had just taken a hurried glance or a quick look that confirmed all of the judgments we already made about ourselves or others. So set the kitchen timer if it helps you, but try to stay with each exercise in this chapter for at least twenty minutes. You can always spend time praying or even doodling if you get stuck in the writing.

Everything in our lives tends to be hectic, and what is subversive about a journaling practice is that it calls us to stop. It is when we stop, when we let our look linger, that a deeper movement within can be discerned. According to journal writer Alexandra Johnson, it is this interior movement that is behind *journal* becoming the verb *to journal*.

We are surrounded by objects in our lives that have stories waiting to be told. They have meanings and purposes that often we alone know about. When asked to write about an object she had and to tell its story, one woman wrote about a couple of pieces of broken shell that she picked up on a Florida vacation and that she keeps in a dish on her windowsill. "To me the broken shells are more beautiful than the whole or 'perfect' ones because you can see the inside of the conch shells, not just the outside. The shell pieces have strips of lovely, translucent color. Seeing them makes me wonder if God looks at me the way I look at these broken pieces of shell—not for the 'perfect' but for the beauty that is there in the broken pieces of my own life. The shell pieces remind me to see the same beauty in the imperfect of who I am and of those around me."

⤳ Object Lesson

> Choose an object that you have had for at least six months, and tell its story. It might be the one thing you would save if you had to flee a fire, or it might be something you rarely take out of your cupboard or closet. It could be a ticket stub from a play, an airline ticket, a threadbare sweater or something left behind from your childhood. Examine this object carefully; hold it if it is small enough. Write about the object in as much detail as you can, and then reflect on its story in the context of your own life.

Commitment to the particular and to the real is rooted in every aspect of our Christian faith. God embraces and celebrates the detailed diversity of the world in creation. Jesus did not simply visit our world or appear as an amorphous, abstract presence. Jesus entered the "real" of humanity—in his birth, in his ministry, in his suffering and his death. As an adolescent growing up in the Christian church, I remember my own surprise in discovering that Jesus was in fact not Christian but Jewish. And that the specificity of his birth as a Jewish male colored everything he said and did throughout his life.

In spiritual practice, noticing the concrete singular can be described as taking a "long, loving look at the real." For example, it is not just that I like sunsets. After all, who does *not* like beautiful sunsets? But I want to tell you about a particular sunset that I saw one evening about six years ago in Berkeley, California, when I was swimming in King Pool on Hopkins Street. I am remembering now that the entire sky over the East Bay was a brilliant orange, and the trees were pitch-black outlines against that red-orange-yellow sky. There weren't many of us lap-swimming in the pool that night, and as a rule, swimmers attending to their exercise are oblivious to what is going on around them. But that evening, one by one we all stopped swimming and took off our goggles to look, to notice, to be amazed at the beauty of that sky and those trees.

To see what is real means to pay attention to our lives, not settling for a generalized or abstract picture. It is realizing that while all of us share the common experiences of birth and death, growing up and aging, each person's pathway through these shared human experiences is unique, shaping her or him as a particular person. The cliché says that the devil is in the details, but I want us to consider whether this might also be where God's presence is known and we learn the answer to God's question, "Where are you?" Our creation as human beings provides a meeting place for humanity and God. Still, it is the details of that creation that take us through the doorway and lead us home.

None of us grew up with generic parents. You had not just any mother or father but *your* mother or father. The mother whose sharp mind can delight and cut with equal dexterity; the father who smokes smelly cigars in the garage and still does not trust you to drive his car. It is not enough to say that your father makes you angry or your daughter drives you crazy—the journal asks for the details. What is it about your dad that makes you feel such anger? Is there something about the way he strides into the room and looks down at you that sets your teeth on edge? What does it feel like to have your teenage daughter say to you (as mine once did), "You embarrass my soul"?

⋙ A Relationship's Story

In relationships, common mathematical principles falter. One plus one always equals three, and the third is the relationship itself. I do not experience just my story or the other person's story, but our shared story. Sometimes this third story is named as a marriage or a friendship, but even if we have no name for it, there is a third story created between a mother and a son, a daughter and a mother, a sister and a brother, a grandparent and a grandchild, a teacher and a student, a pastor and the chairperson of the church. I want you to narrate this third story—the relationship that exists between you and the other person, this place that you both share in, who you are together. This is the story that might also be seen by a keen observer, such as a mutual friend who offers his or her own perspective. Remember, this is not a description of just your feelings or the other person's feelings but an exploration of what happens in the space between you.

For your journal to give you this long, loving look at the real, you must begin by really looking—not just with your eyes but with your whole self. This means that you don't begin by analyzing or interpreting, by arguing or defining, but by *being with*. Stand out in the rain, let the hot sand ooze through your toes, smell the mold in the forgotten Tupperware container, hear the door slam, taste the saltiness of your own tears. Feel the warmth of the fireplace, even if that fireplace exists in the snug cabin of your own imagination. When we really look, we become part of, we are one with. I don't analyze the water as I swim; I move through it and allow my body and my breath to carry me into it. When I long for God's forgiveness, I don't wonder about which doctrine of the atonement might be correct; I link my hand with the hand of the crucified Christ and look into the face of love.

⤙ *Looking Through a Doorway*

> Stand in the doorway of a room from your childhood. It might be a kitchen or bedroom, a bathroom, living room, basement, porch or front hallway. If you stop and reflect for a moment or two, you will see the room. Describe the room in as much detail as you can. Recall that the bedspread wasn't just green, it was bumpy chenille, bright as a lime gumdrop. Describe the collection of perfume bottles on the dressing table and the way they smelled. Notice everything that you see, and then the things in the room that you know are there but are hidden or not in plain sight. If there are people in the room, describe them as well. If others arrive in the room as you write, invite them into your journal reflection, if possible. After you feel that you "have" the room in your journal, note whatever feelings came up during the journal writing—grief, joy, anger, disappointment, wonder, surprise, resignation, sorrow or any other feeling that arose in you.

Above all, this long look at the real must be loving. And that is much easier said than done in our journal writing, as in life. In order to give yourself permission to say it all and name it all in honest detail, you also need to give yourself permission to ignore the enemies of such freedom. These are the two enemies you have probably already met if you have ever attempted or keep a journal. The first is "the Censor," who will try to dictate what you should say, and the second is "the Inner Critic," who will seek to tear down any sense of confidence in your ability to keep a journal at all.

The Censor insinuates himself by trying to tell you what you should say. He interrupts you to inform you that something you want to write is not what you would say if you knew someone might read it. So maybe you ought not to say it at all. The Censor demands that you follow her tedious instructions and color inside the lines. She insists that it is more important to be religiously or politically correct than to speak the truth. The Censor suggests that someone might read what you write, even though you have established a safe, private place to keep your journal. The Censor offers to correct your grammar, spelling and sentence structure for you. But this voice is not your friend. When you feel the Censor hovering around you while you are writing in your journal, denial is not a good strategy. This only provides cover and protection for this insidious voice. Try this instead:

⟫ Silencing the Censor

Recall some unhelpful advice or insistent instruction offered by the Censor in your life, and write it down. If you can, track the words back to their original source. Perhaps a teacher wielded a red pen with impunity or a parent's admonitions seemed to limit the life of your imagination. But even if you cannot find the beginning point, give the Censor a name, and perhaps even a shape or form. When the Censor reappears in your journal giving unhelpful advice, you will better be able to recognize this enemy so you do not let her correcting voice keep you from naming your own truth.

Simply exposing the Censor to the light will diminish its power because lies hate the light. Then you can move away from the presence of those lies or give them to the God whose love for you is so much stronger and more real than the Censor's puny presence.

The second threat to the loving look that is needed in any spiritual practice is the Inner Critic. The Inner Critic's tiresomely repetitive refrain will try to convince you that you will never be able to succeed at journal keeping. It will say that you cannot write or reflect or even remember rightly. This insistent voice chips away at your sense of journaling self-esteem, insisting that your journal is a waste of time.

Sometimes the Inner Critic is so strong we never begin writing at all. We get stuck in a paralysis of perfectionism and procrastination. The Inner Critic will try to discourage you by suggesting that you think about journaling for a span of months, say from now until Christmas, rather than just letting you take one journal entry, one sentence or one word at a time. If you miss even one day of journaling practice, the Inner Critic may convince you that you are never going to be able to keep writing a journal. And that is not true. The Inner Critic will try to get you to hide the vulnerability in writing that we all feel and convince you that everyone else is able to do this without any problem. Seeking to block your own experience, the Inner Critic will try to convince you that what other people say or write is truer, more insightful, clearer. The Inner Critic will say that your own meanderings don't matter or couldn't make sense to anyone else. Again the Inner Critic is wrong.

ᕁ Silencing the Inner Critic

> Beware trying to please the Inner Critic. This will only increase her power over you. Instead try drawing the Inner Critic as the stick figure he is, with lots of cartoon balloons coming out of his mouth, filled with discouraging words. Then tear up the figure and his useless words into tiny pieces and throw them into the garbage.

There is nothing more deadly to spiritual practice or Christian worship than comparing yourself to others, as the Inner Critic urges you to do, or conforming to meet the demands of the Censor. Following these voices will put the focus squarely on your own self-consciousness rather than on your lived experience of the Lord of all the living. In the end, such a focus does not link us with others but isolates us from loving companionship. We all have times of struggle, and we all need to know that we do not write or pray alone but in community with other fallible human beings.

Both the Censor and the Inner Critic will try to isolate us from God's voice that is affirming his love and care for us. But the Censor's disapproval and the Inner Critic's cold stare cannot separate you from this loving presence. The psalmist writes,

> You prepare a table before me
> > in the presence of my enemies;
> you anoint my head with oil;
> > my cup overflows.
> Surely goodness and mercy shall follow me
> > all the days of my life,
> and I shall dwell in the house of the LORD
> > my whole life long. (Psalm 23:5-6)

It is at this table that you may open your journal and say what is true and real. It is here that the cup of your journal will overflow with words and phrases, pictures and drawings that will narrate and illustrate your own life.

4

CLAIMING SIGNIFICANCE

Honoring My Own Story

>━━ ━━<

As a child growing up in a small town in southeastern Wisconsin (population 1,173, as posted on the green sign at the edge of town), I was fascinated by the personal stories I heard on the radio show *Unshackled*. The show was broadcast from the Pacific Garden Mission in Chicago, a ministry located in a tough neighborhood then known as Skid Row because of the down-and-out lives of the men and women who lived there. Most were homeless, and many were alcoholics or drug addicts. The personal testimonies of those rescued by the Pacific Garden Mission usually involved dramatic conversion not only to the Christian faith but also away from a life of addiction that held the victim firmly in its grip—hence the name of the show, *Unshackled*. These addictions imprisoned people in a lifestyle of sin, abject poverty, neglect and abuse. I remember wishing that I had an *Unshackled* story to tell because it would provide the inspiring, dramatic truth my own small life sorely lacked. Then the world would really understand how much I mattered to God—*See how she has been freed!* Then I would certainly know I was saved—*Look at the change in my life!*

By comparison, my churchly life, family troubles and friendship concerns felt insignificant and hardly worthy of my time, let alone God's attention. I knew that "his eye is on the sparrow," but I also knew that an eagle or a parrot or a great blue heron attracts a lot more attention than just one more common brown sparrow. Though I don't think I ever really considered a life of drug or alcohol addiction just so I could have a *real* conversion story, I did wonder what significance my relatively small life could have for me, let alone for the world and for God.

Now I see that this way of thinking was dead wrong. In fact, it was really an insult to me and the God who created me in his image and loved me just as I was. Being named Helen Harmelink and baptized in the Presbyterian church my parents helped to found; living above my dad's corner grocery store; growing up as the youngest of four sisters, but being seven years older than my brother; even the hip dysplasia and the limp it caused—all were essential parts of my own story. As I look back, what surprises and delights me most is the definite shape to it all, the way that the most consequential events in my personal narrative were usually unintended but now seem to be so essential.

I was given a unique set of experiences and a life history that belonged completely to me. Sometimes it is hard for us to claim our own voice with its specific timbre and accent, to walk down the pathway that lies before us, to choose the life that we are given. My own inability to claim the significance of my story might not have resulted in a ruinous life of addiction, as it did for the converts of *Unshackled*. But it did show the same flagrant disregard for the gift of existence that was (and is) given to all of us.

Perhaps it might seem obvious that we claim our personal experiences as we live them each day. But it is often in the retelling that we come home to ourselves in a new way. Sometimes a friend or a counselor or a spiritual director listens until we actually hear ourselves and

see the shape of our own story. Your journal is just such a spiritual
friend and counselor, urging you to say more, tell it all and in the retelling uncover the outlines of your own life—who you are, who your
people are, where you have been and where you are headed.

⌇ Reflections on Your Name

> Write your full name across the top of a blank journal page.
> If you have (or had) a nickname, include that as well. Look
> carefully at those combinations of letters, those words that
> somehow identify you. Think about where those names
> come from and all of the memories, feelings and stories
> connected to your full name. Begin to write openly and
> freely about anything that comes to mind as you reflect
> on your name. Who named you? Have you ever renamed
> yourself? How has your name changed as you have gotten
> older or when you got married? Have your feelings about
> your name changed over time? How are your parents or
> grandparents or distant ancestors present in your name?
> How do you see (or not see) the outlines of your own story
> reflected in your name?

When we can embrace the whole of our story—in its graphic detail, its everyday ordinariness, its inevitable failures, its unexpected
graces and its troubles, small and large—we may be surprised to find
that we begin to see our true self. We might be surprised to find that
transformation means recovering the life we are given in God. One
of the inexplicable mysteries of our free will is that we can claim the
life we are given—or not. We can honor our own story—or not. A
rose does not choose to be a rose, it just is—full of beauty, heavy with
fragrance, dangerous with sharp thorns. But human beings can choose

to be who we are created to be—or not. Human beings are given a choice. Will we be who God created us to be, or will we be who others expect us to be? Or will we be who we wish we were?

A journal is a place to meet your particular life and befriend it. For most of us, such befriending is a way home that requires both faith and trust. Befriending our own lives means paying attention to the meanings and connections that we might otherwise have missed. It might mean naming even hard and difficult truths and finding that the naming itself can begin to break sin's power over us. By attending to our lives, we become better able to make choices in the light of God's love rather than the darkness of guilt or fear or shame. According to theologian Walter Brueggemann, being created in God's image means we human beings can reveal God in the context of our lives. "God is known peculiarly through the [human] creature who exists in the realm of free history where power is received, decisions are made, and commitments honored." We will never show up with integrity, even in a journal, unless we trust and believe that our identity is rooted first of all in our creation in the image and likeness of God.

Jewish author Naomi Rosenblatt writes that many of her childhood neighbors had blue-green numbers tattooed on their forearms from imprisonment in places where they were stripped of their individuality and dignity. "Nothing but the raw power of a deeply rooted spiritual identity enabled these people to survive the camps and reconstruct their lives from the ashes. . . . Faith in our spiritual identity is our best hope for triumphing over cynicism, despair and defeatism." None of us knows what might happen in our lives or in the lives of the people we love. But remembering that we are created in the image of God and given a free will allows us to choose how we interpret and respond to troubles in our lives. When hardships and difficulties threaten a tsunami of destruction, it is our spiritual identity that allows us to find a place to stand. A magical faith believes that the things we are afraid of will not happen to us. But Christian faith admits that the worst things, the things we are most afraid of, could indeed happen to us, but they are nothing to be afraid of. Our courage rises because we know God names us, and our lives—no matter what happens to us—belong to God. We know and believe God is with us in and through it all.

Receiving Our Name from God

Read these words from the prophet Isaiah (aloud, if possible), trusting that the Bible is inspired by God's Spirit not just in the writing but also in the reading. Read slowly enough to allow the words to soak deeply into your mind and heart and seep through the cracks and crevices of your own life.

> But now thus says the Lord,
>> he who created you, O Jacob,
>> he who formed you, O Israel:
> Do not fear, for I have redeemed you;
>> I have called you by name, you are mine.
> When you pass through the waters, I will be with you;
>> and through the rivers, they shall not overwhelm
>>> you;
> when you walk through fire you shall not be burned,
>> and the flame shall not consume you.
> For I am the Lord your God,
>> the Holy One of Israel, your Savior.
> I give Egypt as your ransom,
>> Ethiopia and Seba in exchange for you.
> Because you are precious in my sight,
>> and honored, and I love you. (Isaiah 43:1-4)

Jacob and Israel are names not just for one person in Scripture but for a whole people of God. They are your names as well and are also about your people. Try rewriting the passage in your own journal, or write a paraphrase that includes your own name for Jacob and Israel. If there is a word or phrase that seems especially significant, remain with it and listen for the deeper meaning God might want to give to you in that word or phrase.

Reflect openly and freely about what it means for you to receive your name from God. How has God named you "precious" and "honored" and "loved"? How has God truly seen you and renamed you within your own life? What is the invitation that comes from God in receiving a name? What difference does being named by God make when you are going through a difficult time? Let the journal page hold your response to God, your own prayer.

Part of what compels us to write in a journal is our search for the self that we might have lost or misplaced by following someone else's advice or just getting through life's daily demands. But this is also what holds us back from writing in our journals because then we would have to stop and face all of who we really are, a daunting prospect for many of us. Faced with our own imperfections, we may find ourselves less convinced of God's attentive and unconditional love.

It is almost too easy for us to look to the right or the left at someone else's life and use comparison as a way to significance. Someone else has a better prayer life, another's children are better behaved; their finances are more secure, their marriages seem more romantic; she is more organized, he is more creative. Or we look in the other direction and quietly note that our children are better behaved or successful; we have less debt and give generously to others; we are more organized than she is, more creative than he is.

This way to significance, the way of comparing my life to the lives of those around me, may appear to be less self-focused but in fact always puts me at the absolute center. And it leaves very little room for God to speak into the life that he has placed in my care. After all, my attention is not focused on what God might be saying in the context of my daily experiences. Instead my vision is fixed on how I measure up according to some other criteria. It is not surprising, then, that when comparison with others seeps into our lives, God's presence drains out. Even unconscious comparisons can paralyze us and prevent us from accepting the blessings that God intends for us. But sometimes people break through with their own words of blessing and free us to be at home again with who we truly are.

I stood with my nephew Elijah at the doorway of the Sunday school classroom, looking into a room buzzing with four- and five-year-olds noisily at play. I could feel both Elijah's fear and his hot longing to join them. Elijah had been rejected by his birth mother and had lived in a foster home before living again with his father, my brother-in-law. Elijah's short life had certainly not been easy. This morning Elijah stood still, watching and listening, uncertain whether this place and these children were a threat or a sanctuary for his fearful self. As the anxious, powerless aunt, I stood watching and listening with him. I knew that if I pushed him away, he would press his body more tightly to me, and there would be tears of loss and terror.

Seeing our mutual helplessness and longing, the teacher spoke kindly. "Oh, don't worry," she said, "my own daughter is like that too. She needs to be a watcher before she can be a joiner. Elijah can just stand there and watch until it feels all right. That is perfectly OK." I felt relief and profound thankfulness. Her simple words allowed Elijah to be who he needed to be at that moment. Even more, they gave him the inexpressible gift of acceptance and blessing. We both relaxed knowing that watching was something he could do, a vantage point that allowed him the freedom to join in—or not.

This was how I understood Elijah's dilemma: he wanted to be with the other children and claim that place for himself, but he was too scared and frightened. Standing with him there in the doorway, all I could feel was his fear and my misgivings. But the teacher (like every good teacher, including Jesus Christ), who saw the same longing and fear, framed it in another way. This is how she understood Elijah's dilemma: he was scared and frightened, but he also wanted to be with the other children. She began with the problem and ended with the blessing and hope. Her kind, welcoming words led us from anxiety into peace.

When we look at ourselves or others, we usually begin by saying what is good, add a "but," and then go on to name what is not quite so good. For example, my friend Sally is a very caring person, but she is so disorganized. Or my coworker John can run an efficient meeting and has good office skills, but he just doesn't know how to meet and greet people. What you will remember about this friend and coworker is what you heard last—Sally is so disorganized, and John doesn't know how to meet and greet people. We tend to end with the hard truth. But God, like my nephew's teacher, sees with soft eyes that end in blessing. For example, Sally isn't very organized, but she is such a caring person. John may be uncomfortable meeting and greeting people, but he is so skilled in the office and can really manage a meeting well. When we end with blessing, it changes the way we see ourselves and others. Seeing ourselves and others with the same eyes is both a discipline and a grace. Your journal can be a place to practice blessing yourself and others, and to experience the surprise and grace of a new way of seeing.

Learning to Bless

Try describing yourself in your journal using *but* to separate out what you might see as something good from something more negative. The first time write the description with the "hard" truth at the end. The second time write the description reversing the order of the sentence and writing what you like about yourself, the positive truth, at the end of the sentence. How does this change the way you see yourself? What might it be like to see yourself intentionally through the lens of blessing?

Now describe someone close to you in the same way. Write about them the first time with the hard truth at the end. Then reverse the order of the sentence and write about them ending with what you like about them. How does this change the way you see them? What might it be like for you to intentionally see them through the lens of blessing?

Our creation in the image of God also ends with a blessing: "In the image of God he created them. . . . God blessed them, and God said to them, 'Be fruitful'" (Genesis 1:27-28). The Creator's blessing adds nothing to the creation of human beings. But the blessing calls into existence the potential and possibility of that life that is innate within our very human selves. Blessing defines human reality not out of regret or scarcity but out of fullness and abundance.

This way of seeing through the lens of blessing reminds me of the apostle Paul's instruction to the Philippians: "Let your gentleness be known to everyone. The Lord is near. Do not worry about anything, but in everything by prayer and supplication with thanksgiving let your requests be made known to God. And the peace of God, which surpasses all understanding, will guard your hearts and your minds in Christ Jesus" (Philippians 4:5-7).

5

NAMING THE LANDSCAPE

Mining Below the Surface

 ⌇⌇

When my mother died, my siblings and I went through her things and found her diaries. She had kept diaries for years and years—diaries with four lines for each day and three years in one book. All my nieces and nephews, my brother and sisters, looked up their birthdays and read my mother's record of their births, giving their weight and length and gender. "Bob called this morning and said that Sharon gave birth to a baby girl early this morning. She is 7 lbs. 8 oz.—mother and daughter doing fine. They named her Suzanne Lea. Gray, cloudy day today again." My mother never hid those diaries, nor did she need to; while she faithfully recorded events and the weather, she never wrote about her personal reactions or her feelings surrounding events and circumstances. We all tried to read through her diaries, but we soon lost interest.

The truth was that we were not so enthralled by what the weather was like on April 14, 1967, or when she put her tomato plants in the garden. We wanted to know, or at least know that she knew, about her feelings and reactions to the things that happened within our family. In 1967 I was sixteen years old. I remember that year as a sort of familial earthquake caused by my sister's quick return home from her work in India because of a personal crisis. My mother's daily distress over my older sister's situation and the upheaval that it brought to our family was certainly at the center of everything each day of that year. But in my mother's diary, there is just the faithful notation: "Carol returned from her embassy job in New Delhi, India, today. Went to Mitchell Airport in Milwaukee to pick her up." And again she included the weather report for southeastern Wisconsin.

I believe it was fear that kept my mother always recording only the surface events, as it so often is for me as well. (The old saying is true—"the apple does not fall far from the tree.") It is easy—much too easy, really—to judge her for not sharing her "real" feelings, not naming the anger or disappointment as well as the joy and peace that she experienced. Those treasures were there, hidden in the field of who she was. But she couldn't risk selling the whole field to find them, so she clung to the familiar, the known and immediately observable events around her. She did not share those treasures until much later in her life when my sister-in-law Jill insisted that she write in a "grand-mother remembers" book.

That time, perhaps because she was braver in her older years, my mother began to share not just events but reactions and feel-ings. Interestingly, for this writing she rejected the "grandmother remembers" book with its regimented lines for significant events. Instead she wrote in a simple wire-bound notebook with narrow lines that matched her circumscribed handwriting. In this notebook, she found the grace and freedom to be expansive in her reflections. She began by telling her grandchildren (and all of us) what it was like to go to a one-room schoolhouse and live on Grandpa's farm. She talked about living with her own grandmother and the births of her younger brother and especially her much younger sister, who was entrusted into her care. She told about the few years she spent as a secretary to the first certified public accountant in Sheboygan, Wisconsin, and how much she loved that work. She admitted how difficult it was to leave this job to care for her mother's chronic illness. She told about how her mother's lingering illness affected her engagement to my dad, and about her frustration and sadness about not having a "real" wedding in church because of her mother's illness. She wrote about the financial hardships in the early years of her marriage, and how her father would not lend money to my dad to cover the first mortgage on the grocery store and business he was buying. She spoke then of both her disappointment and determination to prove to her dad that she and my father could make it on their own. She talked about the sacrifices they made as a couple and as a family to pay off the mortgage on the store in just seven years. She never got to write about much more than those first years of marriage and the birth of my oldest sisters. But this is the notebook we read aloud to each other on the days after her death, listening to her share her life with us.

If you are hoping to use the journal as a spiritual practice to lead you into an authentic engagement with God, you (and I) need to choose to go deeper than a diary of events. This is not automatic for any of us—it is a choice. And we will not be able to make this deeper journey into our writing and into ourselves without facing the specter of our own fears. This is true whether it is the fear of failure or success, the fear of doubt or the fear of trusting the deeper truth in our lives. It is this fear that Pat Schneider writes so eloquently about in *Writing Alone and with Others:* "The first and greatest fear that blocks us as writers is fear of the truth we may discover. The world, dressed in our habitual interpretations, is familiar to us.

It may not be exactly safe, but we know how to walk in it. We can get from sunrise to sunset."

We don't take on our fears just because it is the right thing, or as my teenage daughter said, because "we oughta, woulda, shoulda, coulda." We write into our fear because fear is not the enemy of our writing. It is the friend of our writing, and it is often the place where God most wants to meet us. When we are able to enter into our real fears, we find ourselves on the edge of our true desires as well. Every one of us knows that when someone shares from that space, we are walking on holy ground with them. At the intersection of our deepest fear and greatest desire is where God waits for us with the gift of his presence, the hope of grace. Listen to Schneider again: "Where there is fear, there is buried treasure. Something important lies hidden— something that matters—like the angel waiting in the stone that Michelangelo began to carve."

The courage required to face our fears will not come to us because we are brave but because we know we are loved. The reason the angel of the Lord told the terrified shepherds, "Do not be afraid," was simply because the good news of the coming of the Savior, Jesus Christ, meant that love was born in the midst of fear. And when Peter tried to walk out across the water to Jesus and felt himself sinking, he cried out, "Lord, save me!" Immediately Jesus reached out his hand and caught him; love held Peter in his fear, and he was safe. In fact, the most frequent command in the Bible turns out to be "Do not be afraid" or "Fear not."

Only by allowing God's love to meet us at the point of our greatest fear will we move from being people of fear to people of faith. Still, it is one thing to be in theological agreement with the belief that "perfect love casts out fear" (1 John 4:18). It is quite another to uncover our fears and what lies beneath them, trusting that such a perfect, embracing love will meet us there, because the fear itself can hold us captive until we are willing to let go.

๛ *Journaling Focus*

Take a few moments to pray and reflect on the different areas in your own life—your immediate family or family of origin, your work, your faith community, your friends, your enemies or those you struggle to be with, your marriage, your future, your past, your schedule, your body, your mind, or your spirit. Where is God asking you to explore deeper and go beneath the surface of events and reactions? Write down that area in your journal, and why you feel called to reflect about it more deeply.

In the title essay of the book, "Falling into Life," Leonard Kriegel describes the terror he felt when, as a young polio survivor, he had to let go of his crutches and learn to fall down to the mat. Despite the pleas of his physical therapist, Kriegel was frozen with fear. But finally, after days and weeks of refusing, "I found myself quite suddenly faced with a necessary fall—a fall into life. . . . My body absorbed the slight shock and I rolled on my back, braced legs swinging like unguided missiles into the free air, crutches dropping away to the sides. . . . 'That's it!' my therapist shouted triumphantly. 'You let go! And there it is!'" Then Kriegel says, "Yes, and you discover not terror but the only self you are going to be allowed to claim anyhow. You fall free, and then you learn that those padded mats hold not courage but the unclaimed self." When we name our fears and let go, we do not then find courage, but our unclaimed self and God's embrace and love for the very things that caused us such terror in the first place.

☞ *Journaling Focus: Free Write*

Returning to the same topic you chose earlier, spend
ten minutes in a "free write." Write continuously and
without any editing for at least ten minutes. Try to keep
writing without pausing, even if you repeat words or
phrases. When you feel like stopping, try to write a bit
more, asking, what more wants to be told? What remains unsaid?

A daily record begins on the surface, where our lives are lived. The
everyday events matter (yes, even the weather). The details of our
personal map provide a topography highlighting the defining charac-
teristics of the region we call home. The surface relief of hills and
valleys, mountains and lakes, gives us clues about where there might
be something of value to be mined below the surface, in the earth's
darkness. Our journals can function as a sort of divining rod, pointing with surprising, forked words to a reservoir of hidden water or a
vein of gold in our lives. Trust yourself to be more adventurous, and
take time to reflect on your life's surface. Where is God's Spirit asking
you to risk exploring just a bit more? Where does your personal topography indicate faults and fissures beneath even a relatively bucolic
personal landscape? Risk going below the surface, even if it seems
dark down there, remembering the psalmist's insistence that "even
the darkness is not dark" to God and "the night is as bright as the day,
for darkness is as light to [him]" (Psalm 139:12).

☞ *Journaling Focus: Mapping*

Draw a topographical "map" for the area in your life you
have chosen to write about, using whatever kind of map
seems most helpful in representing your own experience.

For example, a literal map could serve to name the "country" where you live, and the roads, detours and topographical details in your personal geography. Or you might make a family tree or draw your church community with the people (including you) sitting or standing in their usual spots. You could use a political map to list the authority structure and relationships of responsibility, helping you see who is—or isn't—in charge. Drawing and naming steppingstones is a helpful way to recall the past or build a pathway into the future. Imagine for a few moments what sort of map might best capture your own experience, and then sketch it out.

All good writing teachers encourage you to begin with what you know. But when we take the step of going deeper, we might begin telling and writing what we know, and then see we really write to *find out* what we know about our own life and experience. Below the surface of a daily record lies a way into what we have not yet understood, but what we can now see or hear or understand. Such self-awareness is not self-indulgence; it is the beginning of wisdom.

If you are writing together with others, you also might find yourself walking further into the underground passage. When our fear of the unknown threatens to halt our explorations, friends remind us that, as in any underground cavern, gold is often best mined in the dark places. Good spiritual companions wear their own searchlights on their helmets as they walk below with us to help us see what is underneath all of our living. And more light means more seeing. Friends can also carry into the cavern an essential mining tool that we often forget—the utter certainty that there is gold to be mined in every person's life—the gold of God's presence, the gift of love. Such shared journaling can be done over coffee with a friend or in a Bible study, a prayer group or a Sunday school class, as long as the setting is a safe place for you to write in your journal and even perhaps read selected parts of your journal aloud. (See the appendix, "Listening Guidelines for a Journaling Group.")

✎ Journaling Focus: Changes

As you explore your personal experience of the area in your life you have chosen, notice how your understanding may have changed over time. Begin a sentence with the words, "What I no longer believe to be true," and respond as truthfully as you are able for as long as you can. Then turn to the next blank page and begin with the sentence, "What I now know to be true," again responding as honestly as you can.

For example, this is how I responded to these sentence beginnings in a journaling workshop: "What I no longer believe to be true is that marriage is easy and comes naturally." After this sentence, I poured out all of the other misconceptions that I had carried into my own marriage. But on the following page I wrote, "What I now know to be true is that marriage is work, but good work; it is work that has, like physical labor, made me stronger and more resilient."

My friend Mandy is a visual artist who often finds it hard to go to the empty white canvas and begin painting when the laundry is still undone. And sometimes it is hard for her to return to a painting that was begun but had to be set aside when urgent matters of family or community or church raised their siren call. After all, her studio does not hold the same urgency as the tasks that need completing or her daughter's five-o'clock pickup from swim team. But she also resists going to the studio because the canvas stretched across the wooden frame is her entrance to both the terror and the wonders below the surface of her own life. One day Mandy walked into her studio feeling a sense of hopelessness that bordered on despair. Then she took all of the to-do lists in her life (and they were many) and made a visual collage out of those lists on the empty canvas. At first all she felt was her own lack of accomplishment, both in completing the lists and in her frustrated desire to paint. All that stuff on the surface of her life was just piled on top of each other, confusing and confounding her life. But then she stood back, in the way that artists do, and she saw what she had missed all along. Below the surface of all of the lists was a life her life—full of people and purpose, mystery and meaning, chaos and connections, emptiness and abundance. And what she felt was gratefulness—a response that surprised her and brought her to her knees.

⤙ *Journaling Focus: Invitations*

Sometimes as we reflect deeply, we realize as my friend did that there are prayers to pray. But the invitation might just as well be to move in a new direction, make amends with someone or find some outside help to get through a tough spot. Perhaps there is a letter that needs to be written, whether we choose to send it or not. What is God's invitation to you in this area, with these people or in this place?

My own writing often surprises me in the same way, giving moments of clarity and insight even into situations that make me frustrated and angry. Sometimes what is revealed is not so much a solution

to a difficult situation as it is a deeper longing for hope and a desire
for a blessing. After a particularly frustrating meeting with my own
supervisor I wrote these words:

> but . . .
>
> I came into the meeting in the early afternoon,
>
> longing for a yet . . .
>
> reaching for a perhaps . . .
>
> straining to discern a maybe . . .
>
> nevertheless . . .
>
> the ellipsis eluded extension.
>
> Doctrine enforced.
>
> Case closed.
>
> Elliptical dots only periods.
>
> Repeated *ad infinitum*.
>
> still . . .
>
> dissatisfied, unfinished,
>
> demanding . . .
>
> show me your backside, Yahweh . . .
>
> the but . . .
>
> hope against hope . . .
>
> blessing against blessing.

6

LISTENING BEYOND WORDS

Blessing the Body

>ᴚᴚ ᴚᴚ<

God our beloved,
born of a woman's body:
you came that we might look upon you,
and handle you with our own hands.
May we so cherish one another in our bodies
that we may also be touched by you;
through the Word made flesh, Jesus Christ, Amen.

JANET MORLEY, *ALL DESIRES KNOWN*

Do any of you get insights while you are swimming?" For a moment the question seemed to just sit there in the middle of the table at Café Roma in Berkeley, California, where the morning lap-swimmers at King Pool gathered for coffee. The unexpected question stilled us into remembering as each of us admitted that yes, this experience of insight was a part of our own swimming experience. Sometimes the knowing that came to us in swimming was a mundane reminder of a task unfinished—the cat's litter box not cleaned, a bill gone unpaid, a promised telephone call not made, an e-mail postponed and not returned. But there is more. Most of us have also experienced the insight of finding a way forward where there had seemed to be no way—a way through conflict in a relationship, an understanding of a dilemma at work, an approach to a dreaded future appointment.

In some inexplicable way, the repetitive lift of arms and head, the regular breathing in and out through mouth and nose, the legs kicking and the body itself moving through the water and through the rhythm of lap-swimming, allows deeper truths to be understood. It is as if the knot that has grown tight within me is loosened by the repetitive motion. As the knot eases, I am freed to hear what was there all along. For me, sometimes it has been the voice of God's own Spirit speaking within my body but gone unheard because of the rising volume of my own fears or life's endless distractions.

When I began journaling after a long time away from this practice, I usually exercised before I wrote. Beginning my journaling with physical exercise seemed to relax the muscles in my shoulders and back, giving me more room to breathe. Usually filled with thoughts that seem trapped within my head, I was able from the beginning to let thoughts and feelings flow to my hand and onto the page with an ease that surprised me. I still find that if I exercise before I begin a spiritual discipline such as journaling, I am more present to myself and my feelings and better able to listen to the movement of God's Spirit within me.

Journaling After Physical Exercise

Whatever form of physical exercise you do most regularly— running, walking, swimming, biking, hiking, aerobics, yoga, lifting weights or working out on a fitness machine, just to name some possibilities—try journaling soon after you exercise. Do you notice a difference in the way you journal, an ease in writing or drawing, new insights and understandings that come both as you write and perhaps as you exercise as well? Reflect on how this might affect your own pattern of journaling as a spiritual practice.

Tristine Rainer writes, "The body doesn't lie. If you can articulate the feelings in your body, present or past, you can generally reach your own complex truth." Though we may be able to manipulate the body's truth with our minds, the body is always the truer witness, less capable of rationalization, denial and excuse, wanting to offer us its more authentic voice if we can only find a way to listen. Every spiritual practice, including journaling, begins with our embodied self. The presence of the body, whether well or ill, physically challenged or physically fit, is inescapable. Without the hand holding the pen or the fingers on the keyboard, journaling remains something that we think about or an ideal that we hope for rather than the reality of fingers turning thoughts to words and meaning and reflection. It is our bodies that open us up to God in prayer.

Sometimes the very word *spiritual* has made Christians believe that they can ascend to a realm of the spirit, transcending the body. But both the Old and New Testaments insist that we cannot come to God and leave our bodies behind. It is part of our very creation as humans. For at our very beginning, "the Lord God formed man from the dust of the ground, and breathed into his nostrils the breath of life; and the man became a living being" (Genesis 2:7). When we say we are human, we are speaking about being connected as bodies to this earth. Even the name of the first human being, Adam, claims this heritage of earth and dust and breath in the creation story. The Hebrew word *adamah* literally means "of dust from the ground."

Lest we think this is just some Old Testament notion that is not relevant to New Testament believers, the Gospel of John insists that Jesus became *flesh* and dwelt among us. It is this flesh that we celebrate as Emmanuel, God with us—God in human flesh, born of a woman in the same messy, painful way we were all born. And lest we think that Jesus came to lead us into some higher realm where we could forget our bodies, Jesus' own ministry seems to be so much about the body—healing and holding and touching, once even mixing his own spit with dirt to bring the miracle of sight to a man born blind (John 9). All the Gospels insist that the Christian faith finds its most exquisite expression in the resurrection of the body. Jesus himself links his own wounded, crucified body with his resurrection body, sharing meals with the disciples so they would know without a doubt that he was not an ethereal ghostly sighting but a bodily presence.

The apostle Paul, echoing both God's creation and Jesus' incarnation, writes to the Corinthians: "Do you not know that your bodies are members of Christ? . . . Or do you not know that your body is a temple of the Holy Spirit within you, which you have from God, and that you are not your own? For you were bought with a price; therefore glorify God in your body" (1 Corinthians 6:15, 19-20). When Paul speaks about the body of Christ, he is not speaking metaphorically. In a dualistic understanding, as the Corinthians had, the body and the spirit are in a forced marriage of sorts, in which the body is more foe than friend. But in the Christian faith, Jesus identifies with this fleshiness, materiality, sensuality and passion. We cannot be the body of Christ in any way that makes sense unless we live out that life in our bodies. The Spirit of Christ and our physical bodies are so intermingled that any attempt to separate the two ultimately debases one or the other.

If our journaling is connected with our bodies, then the thoughts and feelings, the prayers and insights that we record there need to be incarnated in our bodies, just as Christ was incarnated in a body. It is all well and good for me to pray for my niece who has cancer or a friend who is mourning the death of her spouse or my brother, who lost his job when the company he worked for downsized. But Christian prayer is always incarnated by bodily signs of love and concern; our prayer needs our flesh. Perhaps praying in my journal might also mean accompanying my niece to her chemotherapy appointment, holding my grieving friend's hand or sending news about a job opening to my brother.

⤳ Praying with Our Bodies

Take a few moments to remember the people and places that are at the center of your own prayers. List them in your journal and pray for Christ's compassion to be present with them. How might you be called to embody your hopes and longings for these people or these places that you love? Perhaps it is as simple as a telephone call, a card, choosing to be quiet or speaking up for someone. Write this "embodied prayer" in your journal as well. Once written, such prayer will continue to work within us, leading us to follow through on our own prayer.

In spite of all of the convincing biblical evidence, we Christians often remain highly ambivalent about our bodies and even the everyday rituals that give our body life and respect and honor. Washing, bathing, touching, dressing, eating and exercising the body can become chores done with little or no notice. On a deeper level, there is perhaps an awareness that any practice that honors the body can also be used to demean it as well. For example, our sexuality can lead us into an intimacy that speaks of God's own presence, but it can also lead us into ways of expression that debase us as well as those around us. When faced with this ambivalence, our first tendency as Christians is often to deny and repress all of these bodily conflicts. Unfortunately, denial simply heightens conflicts that will not go away. Denial itself is not a pathway to freedom, but instead leads to addictions of all sorts. And addictions, just like healthy practices, are rooted in what we take into our bodies or what we do not; in what we do with our bodies or fail to do with them.

This conflict will not be resolved by denial. The challenge instead is to honor our bodies, caring for their vulnerability. We don't just *have* bodies, we *are* bodies. By extending compassion and blessing to the very parts of our bodies that we might otherwise choose to deny, we begin to see our bodily selves in new ways.

Stephanie Paulsell tells a story of bodily blessing begun in one generation and carried on into the next. When this particular mother was a teenager, she was plagued by outbreaks of acne on her face. One day it seemed so bad to her that she was unable to leave the house and go to high school. Her father led her into the bathroom and asked if he could teach her another way to wash. "He leaned over the sink and splashed water on her face, telling her, 'On the first splash, say, "In the name of the Father"; on the second, "in the name of the Son"; and on the third, "in the name of the Holy Spirit." Then look up into the mirror and remember that you are a child of God, full of grace and beauty.'" Remembering her father's compassion, this same woman, now a mother, teaches her own daughters to sing blessings over their bodies. She reminds them that they are children of God and it is God's image that shows through their bodies.

My guess is that most of us were not taught as children to bless our bodies, especially those parts of our bodies that seem least desirable.

But I can't help but wonder what it might have meant for us if we had been taught to befriend our bodies rather than bemoan or ignore or deny what we least like about them.

∿ Blessing Our Bodies

> Most of us have a part of our body that we would rather hide than recognize. It might be what we believe to be our weak muscles or our fat thighs; our too curly or too straight hair; something we find wrong with our nose, mouth, eyes or skin; our height, our weight or the sound of our voice. It could be disfigurement caused be genetics or disease, or perhaps it is age. If you were to give this part of your body a voice and a page in your journal to speak, what might it say to you? Try saying a blessing over your body, taking special care to extend the blessing to the less desirable part, reminding it that it is full of beauty and grace. What are some ways you could show compassion and care and honor to your whole body?

It is only now in the second half of my life that I have been able to look back and realize that the limitations of my body can become a pathway to experiencing grace and the presence of God in my life. Acknowledging my own relatively small disability has helped me to remember a bodily story that I had buried under my own amnesia of denial, though it is a story filled with compassion and wisdom.

The story begins when I was six years old and I sprained my ankle. My parents noticed that after the ankle healed, I continued to limp. They took me to the family doctor, who sent me to an orthopedic doctor. The diagnosis was that I had a hip dysplasia, sometimes called a dislocated hip. It was a congenital deformity of the hip socket, and in my case it made the hip joint unstable. Because it had not been diagnosed when I was an infant (when the treatment would have been relatively straightforward, if uncomfortable), I began a long series of surgeries to correct the deformity, though in the end they did not take away the limp completely.

I readily admit that those hospital stays were difficult for me, as well as for my parents. But I will also tell you that this experience became a means of grace for me. For a long time I refused to admit this, believing that my role was to deny and overcome any physical handicaps that were mine. But receiving my body as it is has allowed me to recover in my own journal a story of grace that was born not in the body perfect but in the body maimed, defective and utterly glorious.

"Oh, it won't be so bad," the orthopedic doctor assured me with a blithe smile. "You'll be able to start high school with all of your classmates, and the leg cast will only be on for six to eight weeks." Clearly he was not seeing what I saw ahead of me. What I saw was six to eight weeks of slowly, laboriously going up the stairs one at a time with my stronger, more dependable leg encased in rigid plaster, while the other kids pushed past me. I envisioned six to eight weeks of hobbling into every class late, and that long pause as each teenage head would turn to look at me while I limped over to the only available desk in the corner farthest from the door. As I glimpsed my certain fate, asking for a bed on the adult floor of the hospital rather than in the children's ward seemed nothing more or less to me than the plea of a martyr who bargains for the firing squad over being burned at the stake. Even then I never expected my modest request would be granted. I was surprised when the admissions coordinator announced that my room was on an adult medical floor.

There in the fourth-floor dayroom at the end of the corridor, I was welcomed by a group of veteran hospital patients. I was the one with the cast from my hip to my ankle and the bitterly uncooperative stance of a fourteen-year-old enduring her seventh orthopedic surgery. Oddly enough, it was my aggressively bad attitude and my extensive hospital experience that allowed me entrance into this group of the physically maladjusted. But these battle-scarred patients were unimpressed with my hospital history, topping each of my stories with illness stories of their own, many of them beginning before I was even born. In five short days, I came to love this community of the used and abused, the injured and the maimed. Among them I was a peer among adults and recognized as a person with my own integrity, experience and story. It seems obvious to me now that the less-than-perfect bodies of my hospital companions were Christ's body, broken for me and me for them. Only through this less-than-perfect body would the image of God be expressed in my life. From the fourth-floor dayroom, I caught a glimpse of living as an adult with a noticeable limp and a significant hospital history.

⤳ *Telling Your Body's Story*

Let your journal be a faithful listening companion as you recount your body's story. Try listing significant events by periods of five or ten years, depending on your age. These might include difficult events, such as a childhood experience of unwanted touching, an experience of name-calling or an eating disorder; but also include joyful events such as realizing that you are a runner, learning to play soccer, giving birth to your first child or hiking up a mountain. Look back over your list, noticing what has (or hasn't) happened, significant themes and identity issues. How do you feel about your body's story? What part of the narrative still remains to be written?

If, as the apostle Paul entreats us, we are by God's mercy and grace to offer our bodies as "a living sacrifice, holy and acceptable to God" (Romans 12:1), then each of us needs to find a way to offer to God the imperfect bodies we are given, the bodies that we care for imperfectly—our human bodies. Paul seems to suggest it is only through this offering that we will discern the will of God. Perhaps it is only through embracing fully our very human selves that we can come closer to the One who shared our human flesh, who gave it all the honor of God's own presence. Janet Morley offers this prayer:

Loving Word of God,
you have shown us the fullness of your glory
in taking on human flesh.
Fill us, in our bodily life,
with your grace and truth;
that our pleasure may be boundless,
and our integrity complete,
in your name, Amen.

7

LOOKING BACKWARD

Reflecting on the Past

It is not enough to say that each of us has a story to tell; the deeper truth is that each of us *is* a story. A friend once remarked that we travel into the future with bags that we ourselves have packed. I remember agreeing with her and then observing that some of those bags are also packed for us by circumstance and family, gender and gift. It is interesting and enlightening to talk with a friend, sibling or spouse and realize that though you traveled together in the same familial places, the experiences you carried from that place are not at all the same. And not only do people remember different experiences of a shared past, they also can attach very different meanings to the same experience.

Being willing to unpack that suitcase and see what we have carried from the past, rummaging around among the clothes we wore, the songs we sang, the places we walked and the people we knew, is part of this backward look for all of us. As the story is told and retold, we attach meaning and significance to things and events, feelings and insights, people and relationships. Memory is the way we piece together the past in a way that gives meaning to our present experience. It is also the primary way we hold on to our Christian faith in a sometimes threatening and often forgetful present.

It is often surprising to find that as we remember in a journal, the things that once seemed insignificant suddenly take on new meaning. I remember again touching the papery skin on the hand of an older neighbor, seeing the hawk carried on the current of the wind, hearing my nephew read aloud his original story about a "porky pine named Spike." Other things I thought were important for my life's journey now seem to be taking up valuable space. Is feeling snubbed by a careless friend worth holding onto, or is her apology a call to forgive and let go? Memories that I mislaid now are essential gear to get through the day. How could I have forgotten the joy of hearing the words "It's a boy!" just because that infant son is now a lanky teenager with a mercurial disposition?

Making a record of our own particular slant on the past is a compelling reason to continue in a journaling practice. We each need to remember because "each of us must possess a created version of the past. . . . We must acquiesce to our experience and our gift to transform experience into meaning." This urge to "transform experience into meaning" is at the heart of journaling. It is also at the heart of the biblical instruction to remember. Intentionally inviting God into our remembering allows our journal to not only be our friend and confidant but our gentle teacher as well. For Christian believers, recalling the stories of how God has met us along the way of our life's journey is central to our ability to share our personal testimony and is essential for truthful witness.

The prayer of examen, first popularized by Ignatius of Loyola in the sixteenth century, has been adapted over the years to provide a pathway or model for inviting God into our remembering. I have sometimes called the examen "backward prayer" because its pattern helps us to see where we have been and how God met us during our day, as well as those places where we might have missed out on being with God. All the adaptations of the prayer of examen include an invitation for God's light and look to illumine our lives. As a spiritual practice the examen is meant to gently teach us how to see our own daily life as a means of grace. Perhaps this is God's intention for all of our journaling as well. Listen to how Susan's journal helped her to learn about a new way of seeing her life with God.

> I have struggled for a good part of my life with the idea of God loving me. Many times in my life, I have felt abandoned by God and so had embraced an oh-look-how-God-has-failed-me mentality. After reading Psalm 103 one day, I journaled on this struggle of mine to accept a God who carried me every step of the way. "[He] surrounds me with love and tender mercies. He fills my life with good things. My youth is renewed like an eagle's." I found that I wanted to write those words again. And again. It was surprisingly soothing. Such words in the past had only indicted me of the absence of a loving God in my life. I had spent literally weeks writing in my journal of despairing of God's caring presence. The comfort I now found in the embrace of God's love was a small step that turned me quietly away from my own judgment and toward the embrace of God's love.

Like Susan, I am often mystified by my own personal reluctance to remember, despite the clear wisdom and biblical mandate to do so. But the truth is that this looking backward can be pretty scary stuff for us unless we remember that God loves us first and came in Jesus Christ to bring us life. And this is true no matter what has been done to us or what has not been done, what we did or did not do. That love is not conditional, and nothing we do can alter its certainty or change its total acceptance of us as we are. Love's only requirement is that we receive it. God's tenacious love frees us to face ourselves honestly. When we can stand and pray in this truth, we will find the boldness and courage to remember and discern our past.

⤳ Praying for Light

The examen always begins with a prayer for light—to quite literally look at our own lives, as much as we are able, through the light of Christ's Spirit. This is essential because there are two great dangers in praying through our own memory. The first is that we might romanticize the past, becoming either sentimental or nostalgic about "the good old days." Consequently, we would be unable to see the truth of a less-than-perfect self or circumstances. The second danger is that we might demonize the past as essentially unredeemable and recall the past only to remember our own wounding or the ways we wounded others. When we hold tightly or even hide those wounds, it makes it more difficult for God's transforming love to bring us hope.

Without such a view of the past, we would miss out on any possible blessing that might come out of even painful memories. With our eyes illumined by Christ's Spirit, we can see how we often fail as human beings; we miss the mark, get off track and find ourselves in sin. But God's love and forgiveness is unconditional and constant.

Begin by bringing into your journaling space a sign or symbol of Christ's light with you. Some people use a candle or a cross; for some, a rock or fresh flowers helps them to find this graced illumination or reminds them of God's constant presence. What would remind you of the illumination of God's Spirit at the heart of this prayer?

After beginning with a prayer for graced memory and understanding, the examen moves into a review of the past that is rooted in gratitude. Often it is the prayer of the body that helps us to replay our day: "What did we taste and smell, touch, hear and see?" This look of thankfulness need not be long, but it needs to be specific, not general—the acidic taste of this morning's orange juice, the piano's tumbling notes and the singer's confident voice, the nuzzle of the dog's warm body, the look in the eyes of a friend as he recounted a story. Gratitude changes nothing about the circumstances of our day, and yet looking with gratitude can change everything we see. "Like the Israelites who 'dis-membered' (took apart) the events of their past in order to re-member (put it back together) in light of God's caring presence, we too benefit spiritually by telling our life stories with God's faithful love as the unifying theme."

Recently a friend and I were driving along the freeway when we spotted a license plate that seemed to be a single word. Was it *thankfulness*? We sped up a little so we could read the license plate. Then we clearly saw that the word was not *thankfulness* but *thanfulness*. "Well," I said, "they probably couldn't fit that whole word on the license plate." My thoughtful friend was quiet for a bit. Then she said, "I think that a lot of my life I live in 'thanfulness'—less than, more than, better than, worse than—rather than in thankfulness." I nodded my head as I thought of how easy it is to fall into thanfulness rather than thankfulness. The examen is meant to lead us out of the scarcity of thanfulness and into the abundance of thankfulness.

⌒ Looking Back with Thankfulness

A gratitude list is a good way of letting your journal teach the simple lesson of abundance. Write down five things that you are grateful for, no matter how small. Here are some items on my list:

- The smell of lilacs overflowing into the street as I rode my bike to work

- A student who came back to see me after graduating

- A sympathetic e-mail from a friend

- Being able to wear sandals again in the warm weather

- The taste of a perfectly ripe mango

Recording a gratitude list in our journals reminds us of life's gifts that sometimes go unnoticed. "Full of surprises, journals help us bear witness as well as astonish. In doing so, they are like found money."

Then we review the feelings and thoughts and actions of the day, asking ourselves, what rises to the surface and catches my attention? What do I see or notice in my reactions and responses during the day? Naming a feeling that came up or highlighting an action that we took or did not take, an insight that we understood or missed, brings focus to the prayer of awareness. It stops us here at this place in our own lives that we might have passed over or forgotten but now plainly see. It is a daily reminder that God comes to us, and we respond to God, in the particularity of our own experiences of graces, temptations, actions and reactions.

Stopping for a closer look at a remembered feeling or insight and taking time for reflection might seem unfamiliar or irrelevant or, at the very least, inefficient. Many of us live our lives like stones skipping across the water, congratulating ourselves on how many skips we make before our rock slips below the surface. But what if we stopped long enough to let the rock find the bottom and see the water ripple out on the surface? What if we waited long enough for the ripples to end and the water's surface to return to a state of calm? The prayer of the examen seeks to pick up a single rock from the landscape of our lives, throw it into the water and let it sink to the bottom.

⤳ *Praying into the Heart of Our Day*

The prayer that arises out of naming the rock, picking it up and throwing it into the water might be a song of praise or a prayer of lament or a cry of conviction. It could be a longing for forgiveness or a plea for healing in ourselves or a loved one or in the world. The prayer need not be long, only long enough to name what is true. It needs to be long enough to acknowledge where we experienced God's grace and transcended our own smallness, where our sin found us out, where God's mercy overflowed and overwhelmed.

Is there one moment that stands out among all of the moments of the past day? It is often true that our feelings can be an indication of where the action is. Take a moment to stay a bit longer with the strongest feeling from today. Was it the sadness you felt when you realized that you disappointed a friend? Was it the sense of well-being you felt after exercise? Was it the fear that overtook you as you faced a big project at work or a problem at home? Whatever that feeling, stay with it a bit longer and hear the story under the feeling. How might you pray this? Would it be a sigh of sorrow or an exclamation of joy? Would it be a prayer of thanksgiving and praise or a song of loss and lament? Again, this is not about carefully written prayers but about calling out to God. Sometimes when we run out of words, biblical psalms can provide both the feelings and the words that might elude us. Don't hesitate to write a psalm in your journal and paraphrase it to reflect your own situation.

During a particularly painful time in my own life, I discovered Psalm 70. Surely I had read it before, but as I experienced a painful betrayal, the words became my own. The psalm begins with a cry: "Hasten, O God, to save me; / O LORD, come quickly to help me" (v. 1 NIV). And then I heard my own unspoken longing—"may all who desire my ruin / be turned back in disgrace. / May those who say to me, 'Aha! Aha!' / turn back because of their shame" (vv. 2-3). What I heard in that psalm was permission not only to name my deep hurt but to pray it. If the psalmist could say those painful feelings aloud, then perhaps I could as well.

Finally, we end the examen by letting go of all the day's hurts and failures and missed opportunities, dropping them into the bottomless well of God's forgiveness. Then we hold on to the moments in which we caught the music of the Spirit and followed Christ's leading in our lives.

✂ Letting Go and Holding On

Tonight I might ask God to help me let go of discouragement that is clouding my vision. Then I could offer a prayer of thanks for being able to listen to my daughter without interrupting her and giving advice. That, too, was grace. What do you need to let go of tonight? What do you need to hold on to? Write that in your journal, and look for answered prayer.

The examen allows us to sleep in the confidence of the psalmist who wrote, "I will both lie down and sleep in peace; / for you alone, O Lord, make me lie down in safety" (Psalm 4:8). And then we are able to get up the following day knowing "O Lord, in the morning you hear my voice; / in the morning I plead my case to you, and watch" (Psalm 5:3).

What the prayer of the examen teaches is not that all of the past is beautiful and happy, as if we can pick and choose to build a Christian testimony only of praise music. Instead it seeks to expand our Christian musical range by helping us to pray even dark and difficult experiences, confident that God's redeeming grace is the theme even in dissonant times.

As God's grace tunes our hearing, we begin to recognize patterns of speech that make us feel helpless or powerless, inner voices that make us act out of compulsion or an attempt to manipulate others. But we also begin to listen for that truer voice in us—the things we say and do that make our lives and the lives of those around us more hopeful and free—the grace notes of a life lived in Christ. Over time, the practice of the examen brings our lives more in tune with God's true intention for us. We discern more quickly when our lives wander away from the theme and get off-key.

Discernment is a popular word these days. It comes from the Latin word *discerne,* which means "to separate, to distinguish, to sort out." Discernment means "sifting through our interior and exterior experiences to determine their origin." We often seem to be more comfortable talking about discernment than we are actually living the examined life. Perhaps this is because living the examined life is not only about simply cataloging experiences. Christian discernment is about sorting out the voice of God speaking into our lives from the cacophony of many voices that we hear, and then choosing to follow that voice.

⤳ Discerning God's Voice

Take time to ask yourself, when I am moving toward God's voice, what do I sense in my body, understand in my spirit or feel in my heart? When I am moving away from God in my life, what do I sense in my body, understand in my spirit or feel in my heart? Someone has said that it is the nature of God to come to the place where we are and say our name. How has that been true for you?

It can be frustrating that our hindsight often seems to b e more accurate in its view, but it is also a great gift because it means we still depend on faith and the larger vision of God as we move forward. But the acuteness of our backward vision is a gift in another way. It helps us to see the heart of the matter—what is true and authentic for us in the here and now, and what is not. Then we are able to find a true change of heart and a change of direction, what in Greek is called *metanoia*. Listen to Cairns's description of *metanoia*'s turning:

The heart's *metanoia*,
on the other hand, turns
without regret, turns not
so much *away* as *toward*,

as if the slow pilgrim
has been surprised to find
that sin is not so *bad*
as it is a waste of time.

Such discernment takes work on our part; it is also an act of grace in us. It is God who calls us forward, cheers us on and helps us to see what is life-giving and what is not, what leads us into grace and glory and what leads us into resentment and diminishment. What we bring is our willing attentiveness to God's voice, speaking in our relationships as well as in the Bible, through our work as well as through our worship in the church. Becoming discerning people helps us to live authentically each day as disciples of Jesus Christ.

The Bible never seems to tire of exhorting us to remember, remember some more and then remember again. God seems to be aware that we are by nature a flighty and forgetful people. Intentionally recalling and remembering will allow your journal to be your gentle teacher. It will be your own Bethel so that you, like Jacob, just might find yourself crying out, "Surely the LORD is in this place—and I did not know it! . . . . How awesome is this place! This is none other than the house of God, and this is the gate of heaven" (Genesis 28:16-17).

The Prayer of Examen
Praying for light
Looking back in thankfulness
Praying into the heart of the day
Letting go and holding on

8

LOOKING FORWARD

Where Does This Lead?

>︵︵<

My mother was a wonderful seamstress who made beautiful clothes for all four of her daughters. Each week she made a pilgrimage to the fabric section of our local department store in Sheboygan, Wisconsin. I often accompanied her on these shopping excursions, running my hands over the fabric on the bolts, looking at the astonishing collection of colors and textures, designs and contrasts. I spent hours pouring over the pictures of dresses and blouses, skirts and slacks, in heavy, oversized pattern books that lay on the tall, slanted wooden desks. I would carefully choose a dress pattern and then match it with what seemed to be the perfect fabric for that particular dress. After finding the dress pattern, my mother would tell the clerk how much fabric she needed. The clerk would cut the fabric from the bolt and give my mother the small, flat piece.

As I watched all of this as a young child, it was a mystery to me how my mother could take that flat piece of fabric and fashion it into something that had form and fit—a dress that would match the picture in the pattern book. The mystery only deepened for me as my mother would lay the fabric out on the dining-room table and cut it up into many smaller, oddly shaped pieces.

But my mother never doubted that she would be able to make that fabric into a dress. From the very beginning, she envisioned the dress that would come out of her skill and creativity. As my mother sewed together the collar section with the shoulder and attached it to the sleeves, I would begin to see what my mother saw all along. The brightly colored dress took its own shape, transforming the fabric that I first saw on the bolt in the store. But the dress would not be completely itself until I wore it. Only after I put it on could the final adjustments be made so the dress would fit my own particular shape.

My mother saw what I desired and helped me to have my desire in a way that uniquely fit me. Hope begins with naming our desires. We Christians often have the misperception that God could not possibly desire for us what we desire for ourselves. But what if God is at least as loving as my own mother, who was willing to fashion a garment that was what I desired and was uniquely fitted for me? The empty journal page is an invitation to explore what it is that you might want. Our desires imply a longing for what is not yet, what we do not have. Desire is also openness to possibilities and to the future. If we did not begin with desire and longing, few of us would hope for anything.

➤ Make a List

Make a list of one hundred things you want to do or be before you die. If this feels too intimidating, try a list of fifty. But follow these instructions: Let your imagination run free. Allow yourself to repeat some items. Postpone the question, "Do I *really* want this?" Don't worry about the practicality of some of your desires.

One woman found herself repeating her desire for a bulldog puppy. When she noticed this repetition and remained with it for a longer time without dismissing the desire as foolish, she recognized a deeper longing. As she repeated her longing for a dog, she was repeating her longing for acceptance and loving companionship that was missing in her own life. When we allow our desires the room to become conscious and available to us, it is also possible for them to be enlarged or expanded or revised. If these desires remain unexpressed, the true core of our longing often goes unnoticed.

⤙ Reflect on the List

Look back over the list of what you want to do or be. What are the wants and desires that are especially life-giving for you, or the ones that are repeated because they matter most to you? Highlight those desires. Then invite God to see these with you. How do you sense that God sees these hopes? What is the longing at the heart of these desires? What are the fears around these desires? Invite God to be with you as you see both your desires and your fears.

Our desires are always present and condition the way we move forward in our lives. Letting our desires into our journal in prayer is a way of sorting them out and going below the surface. In dialogue with God, it is possible for desires to be expanded or corrected or understood in a new way. Such honesty about what we truly want opens us up to new discoveries and change. We may be afraid of the very thing that we want. We may recognize that without forgiving someone, we will never be free of bitterness and resentment. We may find that we do not want to let go of anger that makes us feel strong and righteous. We may find that an addiction is a comfort we are unwilling to release. At those times, it is especially important to pray for the grace that we desire, knowing that the power of God is greater than we are and greater than the power in the world around us. If we pray for the desire to forgive, to release our anger or bitterness, or to let go of an addiction, we become open to a possibility that is not yet ours. We are available to the greater hope of transformation that is ours in Jesus Christ.

Storyteller Megan McKenna tells a parable about a woman who went into a store and found that the shopkeeper at this particular store was Jesus. As surprised as she was to find him there behind the counter, she was equally curious to find out about this "Jesus store." When she asked what she could buy, Jesus explained that she did not need to buy anything; everything in the store was free for the taking. All she needed to do was bring her list to the counter. As the woman walked around, she saw that the store contained not only things and possessions but values and dreams and hopes. The woman had a grand time writing down on her list all the things that she wanted. She wrote down peace on earth and peace with her sister, no more homelessness or hunger, as well as personal fulfillment and some ready cash. When she came to the counter to tell Jesus what she wanted, he leaned down under the counter and brought out a bunch of packets. She asked, "What are these?" Jesus replied, "These are seed packets. This is a gardening store." She said, "You mean I don't get the finished product?" "No," replied Jesus. "This is a store for dreams." Disappointed, the woman turned around and left her list on the counter.

Sometimes, like the woman in the store, we never really embrace our desires and hopes for the future because we are unwilling to plant the seeds that would bring change. Or we are unwilling to wait for the seeds of hope to germinate and take root and grow. One of Jesus' own parables describes the kingdom of heaven beginning as a mustard seed that no one has much hope for. But the planted seed grows into a tree large enough for birds to perch in its branches. Without the planting of that tiny seed in hope, the tree would never have grown.

⤳ Planting Seeds

> Stop and reflect on your own life. What seeds are you planting today, hoping for a glimpse of the kingdom of heaven? Paul names the fruits of the Spirit as "love, joy, peace, patience, kindness, generosity, faithfulness, gentleness, and self-control" (Galatians 5:22-23). Are there seeds of these fruits being planted in your life and the lives of those around you? Or are there other seeds being planted that come more out of disordered, sinful desires?

Just as we have to wait for seeds to take root and bud and flower, so it seems that biblical hope is often found in the practice of waiting. "We wait in hope for the LORD," writes the psalmist (Psalm 33:20 NIV). The prophets echo this same active waiting: "I watch in hope for the LORD, I wait for God my Savior" (Micah 7:7 TNIV). And the apostle Paul, writing to the Christians in Rome, connects waiting with hoping: "If we hope for what we do not see, we wait for it with patience" (Romans 8:25). Waiting is not easy for me, a naturally impatient person. I want to find the shortest line at the supermarket, the doctor who sees me at the time of my appointment, the airline with the best on-time record. But biblically, waiting is leaning forward into the future that God has promised but that we can't quite see yet. It is Mary's cousin Elizabeth welcoming the promised child she cannot yet see but who is the One her own body and the child within her are already responding to with joy.

⤳ *Waiting and Hoping*

A contemplative waiting prayer encourages listening. Think of a concern and then ask this question: "What do I need to know about my spouse . . . my daughter . . . a ministry project . . . a physical or emotional injury?" Try to remain in this waiting, listening posture throughout the activities of at least a week without trying to resolve the questions into solutions or answers. The following week, write the questions again and ask whether or not there is an indication of a new life, a new understanding, a budding of hope, no matter how small.

In real-life situations, expectations can sometimes masquerade as hope. An abused wife might keep "hoping" that her alcoholic husband will stop drinking and hurting her. But she only enables him to continue by not taking action on her own behalf. What she calls hope is actually the expectation that he will change. And she keeps convincing herself that the abuse will not happen again, despite all evidence to the contrary, because she believes in these fixed expectations. Parents who "hope" that their child will succeed academically and get into a top university may be laying an unrealistic expectation that is a burden for the child. Understanding the difference between hope and expectation is critical if we are to allow our future to be shaped by God. Hope longs for good but is able to be flexible about how that good might appear. Expectation grasps at solutions and becomes easily attached to outcomes. When we are hopeful, our imagination and creativity flourish. But when we are locked in expectations, it is easy to turn our picture of the possible future into an idol.

Expectation assumes that everything will turn out as predicted. Sometimes our past experience confirms our expectation. Because of our past experience, we expect that the chair we sit in will hold us without breaking. But there are other life experiences that do not fit the expectations of the past and are not as simply understood. We have two healthy children, and we expect that the third child will be healthy as well. But the child is born with a heart defect, or she has a developmental disability, and our expectations must die in order for us to live in the hope of this particular child. Or a gifted teenage daughter becomes an addict, or a son who was baptized as a child wanders away from his early Christian commitment. Or we ourselves are diagnosed with a chronic illness, and the shape of our life and future changes in ways we never imagined. Our prayer then needs to look toward the God who is not only with us but also is in front of us, forming a future that we cannot yet imagine happening out of our own effort. A father of a drug-addicted daughter called this kind of prayer "hoping against hope."

A mother whose child was born with Down syndrome told me that when her baby was born, a friend told her she was called to the discipline of hope. Her friend said that for most parents of newborn children, hope is a given, a part of the new baby book that records when the first steps were taken and the first words spoken. While I agree that this mother might be called to the discipline of hope, I am less sure that such a discipline is required only of the parents of a developmentally delayed child. As a mother of three children myself, I see now that there were (and still are) times in each of my children's lives when I am called to the discipline of hope.

More than an abstract concept, living in the discipline of hope means living in a place that keeps our hearts soft and willing to suffer pain and loss. But it is also a place where we live in a faith that imagines a future possibility that cannot yet be seen or perhaps even known. It is here that we practice the same faith that we share with

Abraham, Moses and Rahab: "These were all commended for their faith, yet none of them received what had been promised. God had planned something better for us so that only together with us would they be made perfect" (Hebrews 11:39-40 NIV).

➣ Practicing the Discipline of Hope

> In what area of your own life or the life of the world around you are you being called to the discipline of hope? In your journal, list as honestly and completely as you are able the expectations that have been disappointed. What might it be like to continue to live in hope, even if you cannot see or know what the future might bring?

Luke's Gospel (chapter 24) tells the story of two people who walked on the road to their home in Emmaus, discouraged and disappointed about the state of their own world. As they walked down that road, Jesus himself walked beside them, but they were unable to recognize him. When Jesus asked what was wrong, they "stood still, their faces downcast" (v. 17 NIV). Then the whole story poured out of them. "About Jesus of Nazareth . . . He was a prophet, powerful in word and deed before God and all the people. . . . They crucified him; but we had hoped that he was the one who was going to redeem Israel" (vv. 19-21 NIV). Some of the women said they saw a "vision of angels, who said he was alive" (v. 23 NIV). And still other friends saw the empty tomb but did not see Jesus. Then Jesus, still unrecognized, taught them from their own Scriptures that everything that had happened was part of God's intention all along.

But their disappointed expectations still clouded their ability to hope into a new future. Then the two invited Jesus into their home. They received him, and in receiving, they were received. Jesus, who had always been hosted by others, became the host. "When he was at the table with them, he took bread, gave thanks, broke it and began to give it to them. Then their eyes were opened and they recognized him, and he disappeared from their sight. They asked each other, 'Were not our hearts burning within us while he talked with us on the road and opened the Scriptures to us?'" (vv. 30-32 NIV). Immediately, the two got up and turned around to go back the way they came, this time with a message of hope, possibility and new life.

What Jesus did both in his teaching and in his hosting at the table was to help the disciples to "remember forward." When the two disciples remembered forward, a way opened up to the possibility of resurrection, not merely resuscitation, of the past.

Then the disciples ran back from their home in Emmaus to their friends in Jerusalem, the very way they had walked so despairingly before. They had regained their future from the rubble of the past and the death of their beloved master and teacher, Jesus Christ. None of the facts had changed, but in the resurrection, God's future won out over the grief of past events. One proof of Jesus Christ's resurrection can be seen in the energy and imagination of his followers to see another future in God that they had not glimpsed before. Now they were awake, alive to what is and to what might be. They were able to watch and pray for the coming of the Holy Spirit, even though they could not imagine quite what this would mean for them and for their world. But this they knew: if the One who was crucified was now risen, then all of their assumptions and expectations of how things must be were also dead, and hope was alive once more.

Christian hope is not born out of human optimism against all of life's seemingly insurmountable odds. We are not invited by Jesus to join in Pollyana's "glad game" of spinning every negative experience into a positive outcome. Neither is Christian hope found in the triumph of self-confidence or national power. As Christians, we find our personal hope in this story of redemption and salvation. As people of God, we participate in that narrative when we make choices in light of that hope. We Christians are invited, just as the disciples were, to remember forward by looking every day for signs of God's kingdom in the world and following those signs toward a new reality. This is our calling until the day that Christ returns to make all things new.

9

REORIENTING IN
THE PRESENT

Where Am I Now?

⤛⤜

One of my husband's life goals is to visit all of the national parks. Of the fifty-eight national parks, he has visited fifty-three. This includes even such far-flung parks as Dry Tortugas, an island south of Key West, Florida, and an underwater coral reef in American Samoa. Recently he traveled with our oldest son to one of the most remote parks in Alaska, Gates of the Artic National Park. Visiting this park meant driving past a forest fire and then backpacking into wilderness country. After registering at the ranger station, my husband and son needed to use a global positioning system (GPS) or a compass to orient themselves to their starting place and where they were going. Deep in wilderness country where there are no trails, it would be important for them to trust their GPS or their compass and not depend on their own judgment, which can often become clouded by fear or anxiety or misguided certainty.

Writing in your journal as a spiritual practice is really about naming where you are in the present. It is in the now—in the present moment—that we are called to follow God. It is here that we live and move and have our being. To stand fully in the present is the reason we look at the past for understanding. It is also the reason we look forward in faith to what we cannot yet fully see. The present always stands between memory and hope. This is the vantage point from which you understand the past and look forward into God's future for you.

Jeremiah 6:16 reads: "This is what the LORD says: / 'Stand at the crossroads and look; / ask for the ancient paths, / ask where the good way is, and walk in it, / and you will find rest for your souls.'" Asking for the good way at our own life's crossroads means taking a closer look at where we are and where God is leading. A personal compass can be an invaluable tool for such personal navigation in our own lives, especially when we find ourselves in uncharted territory.

⤷ My Personal Compass

Open your journal to a new page. Or better still, use a large sheet of blank newsprint, if you have it. Draw a large circle and divide it into four quadrants representing the four directions: south and north, east and west. In the center draw a smaller circle, and leave this space open as your place to stand and look in each direction. This is an illustrated compass, so feel free to create a collage using color or drawings, magazine words or pictures, or anything else that expresses what you see as you look in each direction.

～ Looking to the South

To encourage your compass to lead you into the joy of personal orienteering in your journal, begin by pointing your journal compass to the south. This is the direction of the sunny exposure—the direction of creativity, imagination, spontaneity and play. Ask yourself: Where do I feel my creativity being called forth? What do I really long to do or be? How do I nurture myself? What are the hobbies I'm passionate about?

Bring your own creative spirit to this playful side of the compass. One person wrote word phrases, and then after reflecting on the words, chose a watercolor to wash over them. Another made a collage of magazine pictures that attracted her. Still another person used photos that illustrated one of her favorite hobbies as well as what nurtured her spirit. When I looked in this direction, I found myself writing the name of a friend who loves sharing fun and good times with me.

Standing at the crossroads is not quite as easy as it might appear on the surface. To stand in the present moment, we need to remember what Moses instructed the Israelites when they left Egypt: "Watch yourselves closely so that you do not forget the things your eyes have seen or let them slip from your heart as long as you live" (Deuteronomy 4:9 NIV). But memory itself can be a powerful force, pulling us backward as well. We are sometimes reluctant to let go of what we know, even if those habits and patterns are no longer life-giving. So if we are to stand at the crossroads and find the good way, we must also heed the instruction of the prophet Isaiah to the exiles: "Forget the former things; / do not dwell on the past. / See,

I am doing a new thing! / Now it springs up; do you not perceive it?" (Isaiah 43:18-19 NIV)

In a similar way, biblical teaching urges us onward, leaning us forward from the crossroads of the present into God's future. The author of Hebrews describes our faith as vigorous exercise: "Let us run with perseverance the race marked out for us. Let us fix our eyes on Jesus, the author and perfecter of our faith" (Hebrews 12:1-2 NIV). We hear in these words the longing of our own heart to be about the urgent business of God's work here on earth. But if this becomes our single goal, we might fill up our lives with churchly activities and ministries of compassion, striving for the goal only to find that it is no longer Jesus ahead of us but a future of weariness and burnout. When we hear the instruction of the psalmist encouraging us to "take delight in the LORD, / and he will give you the desires of your heart" (Psalm 37:4), we wonder what it might mean to delight in the Lord. We wonder, how can I ask for the desires of my heart if I no longer know what I really want?

Looking to the East

Take a look in the easterly direction on your personal compass. This is the direction of the dawn, the rising sun. It is the perspective of new beginnings. Ask yourself: What light is just beginning to appear on my horizon? What am I being asked to take hold of in a new way? Where am I being called to embrace something? What areas in my life need change or transformation?

As you look to the east, remember that beginnings are usually small and can seem almost insignificant. It is easy to miss the budding of something new when other parts of our lives demand our time and attention. So it is important to look carefully and thoughtfully in the eastern direction.

It seems to be altogether too easy to get attached to a single way of being and to lose perspective on the larger reality that God might be calling us to. It is only when we are willing to stand at the crossroads and look in each direction that we are available to God to move in the good way and find rest for our souls. When we stand at the crossroads, we are not attached only to the past or to future possibilities. To truly stand at the crossroads means we need to detach ourselves from all the things around us that promise false security or numb our awareness of the present. We need to let go of all those things that make us feel worthy in our own eyes or the eyes of those around us. Some of us may need to let go of cultural myths about beauty or body image, youth or age. Others might need to let go of perfectionism, outward success or the need for control. Whatever we become attached to—even our youthful dreams or middle-aged disappointments—can stand in the way of being able to choose God and respond to God's Spirit stirring within us and around us.

ᐳᐸᐸ Looking to the West

Take a look toward the west on your personal compass. This is the direction of the setting sun. It is the perspective that shows where there are endings and where we need to let go. Ask yourself: What maps no longer work for my life? What (or perhaps who) needs to be released and let go? What beliefs or attitudes or patterns do I need to die to? Where is deep healing needed? What areas in my life need change or transformation?

Often the eastern and the western directions on our personal compass are intimately related. We may not be able to receive a new beginning and give it the attention it needs to grow and flourish until we let go of something else. One woman realized that there was new growth in her relationship with her husband, but she could not embrace the new beginning without giving up her own sense of disappointment and even bitterness over an experience earlier in their marriage. To accept new hopes would be to let go of past disappointments. Another person realized that because she was still grieving her husband's death, looking toward the east was painful and inauthentic, despite everyone's urging her to move forward with her life.

One way we remain available to God's Spirit is to receive the day—this day, this moment, this season, these people in our lives and the life we are given in Christ. I will be the first to admit that this is not always easy for me. When I look at the givens in my life today—from the gray, January cold of Chicago to the struggles and joys of my marriage or my children or my friendships—it is easier for me to see them as limitations. The limitations I see are my own as well as those of the people around me. Seeing these givens as limitations can make me feel frustrated and angry at myself and others.

But if these givens are seen as gifts, then the choice remains with me. Will I let these gifts move me toward God or away from God's life in me and around me? The key to a gift is not what is given but how the receiver responds and accepts the gift. Am I willing to receive this gift in a way that it becomes part of the continuing story of God's work in my life and the life of the world? Or will I block its unfolding in my life by refusing to accept it? Seeing circumstances as gifts rather than givens changes the way we look at even difficult realities.

I met Caroline while I was working as a medical social worker, shortly after she was diagnosed with advanced colon cancer. Caroline had spent her life caring first for her younger siblings and then for her aging mother. When she was diagnosed with cancer, a brother whom she had cared for as a child stepped in and urged Caroline to enjoy whatever time she might have left to her. Caroline's joys during those months were simple times of freedom and a little traveling, but they were a gift to her. She remarked to me that upon hearing her diagnosis, many people around her began to refer to her in the past tense, "as if I were already dead," she said. I knew that this was not an uncommon occurrence for those who have a terminal illness, and I simply nodded my head in agreement. But Caroline went on to say, "The funny thing is that I have never felt more alive in my whole life. I don't want to miss anything. It is as if all of my living was simply for this moment." Caroline's cancer was a given, but she was able to receive the time after her diagnosis as a gift.

In a similar way, when I volunteered at a medium-security prison, an inmate confided to me that it was only since she had been incarcerated that she felt real freedom. "All my life, I've attached myself to men I thought were going to be my salvation, trapped by drugs that were going to offer me relief from an impossible reality, holding on to unrealistic fantasies that were going to make me live 'happily ever after.' But since I've been in prison, I've found a better way, a good way—maybe what God intended for me all along. I feel like I found myself for the first time. Clean and sober, I'm really free to learn. I am surprised to discover that I am smart and not a loser." This inmate received her time in prison, which was clearly an unavoidable given, as a gift for her. She was able to grow and rebuild her life from the inside out.

None of us would choose to serve prison time any more than we might choose to have cancer. But the key for each of these women was accepting what appeared to be a limitation, even an ending, as a gift.

As you look at the past and ponder the future, what difference might it make if you choose to see the givens of your life as gifts rather than limitations? Might you, too, find in the scarcity of too little time or too little compassion the possibility of abundance and potential? Might you find that you are available to yourself and to God in a new way?

Making a conscious choice to live *with* Jesus rather than live *for* Jesus is another way of being available to God's Spirit in the present. When we live *for* God rather than *with* God, it is easy for us to move ahead on our own steam only to find ourselves resentful or frustrated, exhausted or burned out. Living *with* God means following his lead rather than leading out; it means being in his time rather than our own; it means letting God's love instead of our own effort fuel our actions. All those things that we do *with* God, those that are hard or difficult as well as those that are joy-filled, will form us in Christ as followers of God. But all those things that we choose to do *for* God may be good or even noble and self-sacrificing, but they will not lead to our being formed into the life of Christ. In the busyness that is often the Christian life—certainly the church life and academic life— it is easy to lose sight of this central purpose while accomplishing what seems to be, and often is, good work.

Living with God means staying close to the Word, keeping up the practice of prayer, and living in Christian community. We do this not because it is the "right" thing to do but because prayer and community and biblical foundations help us to see God's presence. Living with God requires us as Christians to live intentionally and attentively. When we seek to live with God, we should not ask the question, what would Jesus do? But instead we should ask, what is Jesus doing in the world? "What we need to have so as to move us beyond our practical atheism is a deeper sense of how God is already present and acting in the seemingly ordinary events of our lives . . . to be able to see the conspiracy of accidents within ordinary life, the finger of God." When we live for God, we might well move forward in self-righteousness, but when we follow God and live with him, we will find ourselves on holy ground, moving in a natural way of humility and listening and love.

⤳ Looking to the North

The northerly direction is really the key to any compass. It gives the perspective that is needed to keep the other three directions aligned and the compass user on course. On clear nights, the North Star remains a navigational tool for smaller boats. On your personal compass, the north represents this guiding light. These are the stabilizing forces that name where we are and point us to a true destination.

Ask yourself: Who is it that deeply loves me and guides me? What are the images or pictures of God that nurture and sustain me? Is there a grace story or salvation story from the Bible that animates me? Is there a grace story or salvation story from my life that is central to my understanding of God or brings clarity to my own life? Who are my spiritual guides and deepest friends?

As you reflect on this northerly direction, it might be appropriate to say a prayer of gratitude for the people and pictures, the words and stories that give hope and a sense of meaning to your life.

Take a moment now to look at all four quadrants of your personal compass. Can you allow God to love you just as you are right now? It is God who gave you this particular life in this particular moment. It is God who wants to love you as you are. Finding God in your life is about knowing that God has fallen in love with you. Following God in your life is about falling in love with God. "Our 'behavior' will not be changed long with self-discipline, but fall in love and a human will accomplish what he never thought possible. The laziest of men will swim the English Channel to win his woman. . . . By accepting God's love for us, we fall in love with Him, and only then do we have the fuel we need to obey."

With our eyes wide open to God's goodness, our wonder returns, our gratitude is rehabilitated and our soul can find a place of rest in the present. What might it be like for us to simply pull out a lawn chair, sit down and rest in God's presence at the crossroads of this present moment? Can we surrender enough to relax and enjoy God's love?

Looking at the Center

Take a look at the empty space at the center of your personal compass. What might it mean for you to put a "yes" at the center and commit all of the directions of your life to God's love? Are you able to say yes to living with God in your whole human person—your heart and mind and body? If you are able, put a "yes" or a symbol of your "yes" at the center of the compass. Be sure to note as well the areas where you might still be struggling to live fully with God.

Our willingness to be with God—in our prayers, in our actions, in our leisure, in our relationships, in our commitments—will lead us in the good way along the path with Jesus Christ. It is a path where Jesus himself offers the invitation: "Come to me. Get away with me and you'll recover your life. I'll show you how to take a real rest. Walk with

me and work with me—watch how I do it. Learn the un-
forced rhythms of grace. I won't lay anything heavy or ill-
fitting on you. Keep company with me and you'll learn to
live freely and lightly" (Matthew 11:29-30 *The Message*).

10

TALKING BACK

Dialogue Journaling

⟩━⟨

The truth is, I enjoyed being a mother of three lively children, with all the challenges of parenting a baby, a toddler and a newly enrolled kindergartener. I also enjoyed the opportunities I had to teach and preach at the church where I was a part-time associate pastor, because I knew that I was living out the gifts that God placed in me. Yet even though I loved my kids, I wasn't having such an easy time loving myself with them. I often felt myself getting irritable and short-tempered. Even though I found personal fulfillment in my church responsibilities, I felt guilty about talking about God to others without having much of a relationship with God myself. I didn't seem to know what I wanted for myself, so it was easy for me to project out to others my own sense of dissatisfaction. Exhausted and upset, my late-night conversations with my husband usually seemed to be about how hopeless things felt to me. Then in a conversation that had every potential of turning into another argument, my husband unexpectedly said, "I think you need a Sabbath."

I became uncharacteristically quiet in response because something about this rang true to my tired spirit. It was a clarifying moment for me. Still I protested, "Sundays are the busiest days of our week because of church responsibilities. And even afterward, there is no peace and quiet. Because our house is such a central location, we always have at least two or three other children coming over after church." All of this was true. Finding a Sabbath seemed to be another good idea just out of my reach. But my husband suggested an evening during the week—"What about Tuesdays?" Then he offered to stay with our children on Tuesday evenings and not let evening meetings get in the way of this responsibility. How could I say no to such a gracious offer?

My first Tuesday-night Sabbath began with swimming at the YMCA, followed by eating dinner blessedly alone and then bringing my neglected journal to one of Berkeley's ubiquitous coffeehouses. I had gone to a journaling workshop at New College–Berkeley earlier in the year and enjoyed it immensely. I had resolved to continue this practice, only to be caught up in the demands of my busy life. My journal had remained on the desk, unopened. But I retrieved it for my evening Sabbath. One of the journaling practices suggested in the workshop was dialogue prayer. Even at the workshop, I was skeptical that this way of journaling could be anything but artificial. But now, looking for a way back into prayer and desperate to hear God's voice, I decided to give it a try.

I freely admit that it felt a little silly to put my name at the top of the page and write to God, "Well, it has been a long time since I've talked to you—in fact, it has been years." Then I wrote on the next line "God" and waited for a response. All the voices in my own head said, *This is stupid, Helen, a pure waste of time. It will just be your own voice ringing in your head.* But true desire fueled by desperation often pushes us into unexpected places, as it did for me that night. So I waited in the café for the next word. After some minutes of silence, I picked up the pen and wrote, "Helen, welcome back, I've missed you!" And I felt my eyes tear up in that coffeehouse because behind those simple words was a warmth and acceptance that I couldn't have conjured up from my own spirit, even out of the most sincere effort.

This began a season of dialogue prayer with God that continued for several years. Once a week, in the same Berkeley coffeehouse, God and I met for conversation in my journal. I filled up one journal and another and another after that. Sometimes it still felt silly, like I was just listening to my own echo. But often enough a word broke through that was not just my own. It had a different timbre and inflection; it was rooted in a love and compassion that I seldom held for myself. The dialogue itself provided a way to God. Out of my own longing for something I couldn't even articulate and didn't know, I refound a relationship with God—and the joyful surprise that God also longed to be with me.

Who knew that desperation could lead me into finding God? All that I brought was my own willingness to receive God's hospitality and respond to an invitation that had been there all along. Now it seems so obvious when I read Jesus' own words: "Ask, and it will be given to you; search, and you will find; knock, and the door will be opened for you" (Matthew 7:7). But such easy access seemed impossible until desperation forced me to risk a new way. Ruth Haley Barton writes, "As strange as it may sound, desperation is a really good thing in the spiritual life. Desperation causes us to be open to radical solutions, willing to take all manner of risk in order to find what we are looking for." And the only risk that I needed to take was trying a way of prayer that was different and felt a little bit silly. What I discovered was not just a helpful journaling practice but a way of relationship that led me back to God's presence.

〜 Dialoguing with God

Write your own name in your journal, followed by a colon.
Then give God an unedited version of how it is with you
right now. Now write "God" or "Jesus" or "Holy Spirit,"
followed by a colon. Set down your pen or rest your fingers
on the keyboard and listen for a response. If you hear nothing or if this seems crazy to you, put your own name again
after the blank space and write, "This feels crazy" or "I
don't hear anything." But don't fill in the blank space next
to God's name until you feel led to do so. Sometimes this
will open a conversation that will continue later in the day,
so you may have something to put in that space then—or
you may not. Try this for at least a week as an experiment
in journal prayer, setting aside, if possible, the Censor and
the Inner Critic who will try to convince you that this dialogue cannot happen or, if it does, cannot be true.

Dialogue journaling is one way of using relationship as a pathway to
knowing God, yourself and the world around you. Ira Progroff is perhaps the best-known teacher of the dialogue way of journaling practice. He insists that what he calls "dialogue scripts" simply allow the
dialogue that is already there to be written. "Underlying these written
dialogues, however, is the more fundamental sense of dialogue not as
a technique but as a way of relationship. The dialogue relationship is
a mutual meeting of persons, each accepting, speaking to, and most
important, listening to the other. This is the I-Thou relationship." The
openness to the "way of relationship" and the underlying dialogue invites us into a heart-to-heart conversation with God our Creator; or
with Jesus, who is Emmanuel, God with us; or with the Holy Spirit,
the Comforter living within each of us.

The moment of risk for us in this journaling prayer is not in our own speech but when our pen is suspended above the paper, or our hands above the keyboard, and we wait for a response. In this moment of listening after we have spoken honestly, we are living out our conviction that God, the Creator of all that is and will be, wants to have a relationship with us. It means believing and trusting that it is both God's intention and longing to reveal himself to us—and ultimately to *me*. This is not some form of holy dictation, as if we could know the mind of God. But it is living out our faith that God wants to reveal himself to all humanity—even to you and me. It is certainly true that any word that is received needs to be tested against the Scriptures, with the community around you, with trusted Christian companions and against your own life experience. But remaining still long enough to listen can give God space to say something surprising or even new.

The way of dialogue can also offer ongoing wisdom at times when we feel alienated not only from God but from trusted friends and mentors as well. We all have wise people in our lives, whose voices have guided us in the past. Perhaps you saw their faces in the northern quadrant of your personal compass in the last chapter's exercise as you answered the question, who are my spiritual guides? They might be grandmothers and grandfathers, mother and father, or spiritual fathers and mothers, an aunt, a neighbor, a friend or teachers. These are the ones whose insights gave us a light of direction and understanding when our own light failed. Often these people can be present to us in ways that are not bound by the constraints of time and place. This happens to us spontaneously when we do or say something and then exclaim, "I can just hear what my friend would say!" These are the wise others whom we know or who live in our memories, and we have incorporated their thoughts, behaviors and values into our own lives along the way.

⤳ Rechecking Your Personal Compass

Look again at the northern quadrant of your personal compass from chapter nine. Is there someone listed there who might offer wisdom about a particular predicament, encouragement when you face disappointment or guidance about how to move ahead with something in your life? Whether that person is alive or dead, you can recognize the sound of his voice or the inflection of her speech. Again, put your own dilemma first, and then listen for a response that seems to carry the tone and speech pattern of this mentor. Allow yourself permission to be a bit skeptical about listening to a person who is not in the room with you—but keep your pen or fingers at the ready to hear and respond to their instruction or comfort.

All journaling, but perhaps especially dialogue journaling, is dependent on the good use of our imagination. Without our imagination, the world would be bereft of story and poetry and much more. When I hear a story for the first time, whether someone is telling it to me or I am reading it, I see it with my mind's eye. I imagine the place, whether it is inside a room, out in the middle of a field, along a lakeside or on a busy city street. I see the people, with all the details of color and dress, facial expressions and mannerisms. Recently I read a novel that took place on the north side of Chicago, much of it in my own neighborhood. Not only did I imagine all the locations in the story, I brought to that book what I had already experienced and knew of the place where I live.

What if we brought that same storied imagination to our reading of Scripture? Picturing biblical stories helps us to really see what is going on. Dialogue prayer with the characters in the story can open us up to truths we might have missed in a surface reading or even in a Bible study. Yet we are often reluctant to use our imaginations to understand the Scriptures. Perhaps we are afraid our imagination will lead us away from the truth; we are not convinced that our imagination could help us perceive a deeper truth. But what if we began by praying that our imagination would help us in our desire to follow Jesus more closely or to sense God's presence more surely? Our imagination might then be a help and not a hindrance in our reading of the biblical story. Through the good use of our imagination, dialogue prayer with scriptural stories gives us eyes to see new sides of the "same old story."

⋙ Dialoguing with a Gospel Story

Begin by praying for the leading and guiding of the Holy Spirit. Then read the healing story told in Luke 5:17-26 several times (aloud if possible), actively using your imagination to see what is going on. Picture the story unfolding. Notice what time of day it is and what the weather is like. Where are people sitting or standing? Where is Jesus standing? Choose one of the characters from the story, or an unnamed bystander, and begin a dialogue by explaining who you are and asking this person whatever questions come to your mind. Listen to what the character says to you, and respond as well. Give your imagination permission to wonder how Jesus was with people, how people felt about him and themselves. After the journaling dialogue, review what you wrote, asking yourself, what did I notice in myself as I listened to the person or to Jesus? Is there something that I may want to say to Jesus or that Jesus wants to say to me? Reviewing your prayer is an important part of the dialogue technique, as it grounds you in the present and your own experience.

During the time when his people were in exile and far from their beloved home of Zion, the psalmist wrote: "By the rivers of Babylon we sat and wept / when we remembered Zion. / There on the poplars / we hung our harps, / for there our captors asked us for songs, / our tormentors demanded songs of joy; / they said, 'Sing us one of the songs of Zion!'" (Psalm 137:1-3 NIV). But it was not just physical exile that they experienced. When asked to sing, the psalmist responds, "How can we sing the songs of the LORD while in a foreign land?" (v. 4). As exiles living in Babylon, the Israelites were exiled as well from their music and from their own sense of hope. Feelings of lament, sadness, anger and even the violent thoughts of many of the biblical psalms arise out of a deep longing for God to see and hear, understand and rescue: "I am worn out calling for help; / my throat is parched. / My eyes fail, / looking for my God. . . . In your great love, O God, / answer me with your sure salvation" (Psalm 69:3, 13 NIV).

When we are exiled, as the psalmist was, from a place we love or people we love, we also need to cry out to be seen and heard. Sometimes we find ourselves exiled from the very things that brought us close to God in the past. Like the psalmist, we can feel exiled from the music of our lives. When people around us try to encourage us to keep on singing, we find we have hung up our musical instruments and our throats are too parched to bring forth a song. But God waits not for a musical performance but for the true cry of your heart. Dialoging about the way you feel exiled by trouble or transition or loss is not simply about inner truth-telling; it is honestly letting God know how it is with you.

Sometimes we exile parts of ourselves that seem less efficient or effective or productive but are truly life-giving. Perhaps it is that passion for writing that you had as a child, or your secret longing to be an artist, fly an airplane, travel to Tibet, climb Mount Whitney or simply have more fun every day. Recently I looked at the southern quadrant of my own personal compass and found again all the ways that I nurture my spirit. I also realized that even though I know these ways, I neglect to take the time to play the piano or set aside time for a card game with a friend. Are there some parts of yourself that exercise power and control while other inner voices are ignored or silenced?

What are the parts of yourself that you have exiled to a hidden place within you? What are the marginalized and lost parts of who you are? What would it be like to open the door and allow these shadow sides to come out and have their say? What would they want you to hear? Could you invite them into the conversation about who you were and are and will be? Building a relationship with marginalized parts of who we are is a step toward a truer wholeness.

Gathering in the Exiled Self

> Name something that is part of you but now feels exiled from you, your life or your personality. It might be a feeling or emotion, an activity or vocation, a place or a person, an insight or a dream. Begin by talking about your relationship to this exiled part of yourself. Then allow this exiled self to find its own voice, to explain what happened and what its hopes are for you.

When you make an honest return to God, and to your true self, you might be as surprised as I was to find God's welcome and hospitality, even for the places within us that we ourselves struggle to embrace.

The way of dialogue in your journal dares you to ask questions, make comments and then listen for a response that might be within us or beyond us. Those words I heard in the Berkeley coffeehouse are there for all of us, and for all of who we are: "Welcome back. I missed you, and I'm glad you are back." If God is so hospitable, even to those parts of us that we find least acceptable or have long neglected, who are we to keep them from speaking? In the end, who are we hiding from anyway?

11

EMBRACING THE CROSS

Finding My Way Through Suffering

>━━ ━━<

The fishermen—Simon and his two partners, James and John—are understandably excited to leave their fishing nets and follow this new rabbi and teacher, Jesus. OK, the truth is, they are all a little nervous. Simon speaks for all of them when he exclaims that he is a "sinful man" (Luke 5:8). None of them are afraid of leaving their old lives behind. But they all feel unworthy of becoming the disciples of a rabbi who already demonstrated miraculous power by filling their empty nets with fish. Jesus reassures them all when he says, "Do not be afraid; from now on you will be catching people" (v. 10). Who could turn down such an opportunity to change their lives and learn from the rabbi? Who could doubt the confidence that Jesus had in them? So they pull their boats up to the shore and leave everything behind to follow Jesus Christ.

For Simon and the other disciples, following Jesus is not just about learning knowledge from a gifted teacher. It is about becoming like Jesus; they longed to be what Jesus already is. They want to walk in the footprints of Jesus so that their steps will match their Master's gait and direction and journey. Wherever Jesus goes, they will go. What Jesus does, they will do. If Jesus heals the sick and the demon-possessed, then they also will heal the sick and the demon-possessed. Jesus does not argue with their perception but invites them along, not just to know what he knows but to do what he does and go where he goes. Sometimes the depth of the disciples' own prayer is lacking, and they are unable to heal. Or their faith in their ability to follow Jesus out onto the water falters. But Jesus continues to urge them forward, and they continue to follow him in their stumbling, bumbling, human way. That is, until Jesus suggests that they must follow him to his own suffering and death.

When Jesus explains to the disciples this part of his journey, Peter insists that there must be some mistake: "God forbid it, Lord! This must never happen to you" (Matthew 16:22). But Jesus' own reply to him is swift and devastating, "Get behind me, Satan! You are a stumbling block to me" (v. 23). Peter and the disciples are literally standing in the way of the journey that Jesus has chosen. Their own human concerns for survival are standing in the way of the larger concerns of God for Jesus to embrace suffering as part of the journey toward life. Like all good teachers, Jesus repeats again and again what lies ahead for him, and the disciples are filled alternately with denial, grief, bravado, anger and disbelief.

Then the disciples' worst fears are realized. Jesus chooses to walk into this unavoidable and unfair suffering. Jesus receives a kiss that is not intimacy but is betrayal by one of his own. There is a court and a trial, but there is no justice. Jesus experiences suffering and pain; there is no compassion. Instead Jesus is ridiculed, mocked, scourged and marched by force to his own execution site. Even while on the cross, there is only sour vinegar offered when he thirsts. The soldiers strip him and cast lots for his robe. Unable to face such hard suffering, most of the disciples simply flee. The execution itself is a long and painful death on a cross. After the sword pierces the side of Jesus, his lifeless body is taken down from the cross, wrapped and placed in a tomb with a large stone rolled into place at the entrance.

As their world shatters, the followers of Jesus are sure of one thing—Jesus, their Master, is truly dead. The excitement they felt when they left their nets to follow him is replaced now by embarrassment and shame. Neither hero nor savior nor redeemer, Jesus is instead a common criminal, convicted as a blasphemer and executed. The expectations for their journey with Jesus are now entombed along with the body of their Master.

Like the disciples who surrounded Jesus, our first impulse when we face suffering is to flee or deny the suffering around us or within us. But what if experiencing our own sorrow or the sorrow in the world around us is a pathway into the heart of God? At these inevitable times of suffering and death, Jesus Christ's own journey through death, entombment and resurrection provides a journey that can unite my life of suffering with Christ's own suffering. Walter Wink writes,

> Jesus at his crucifixion neither fights the darkness nor flees under cover of it, but goes with it, goes into it. He enters the darkness, freely voluntarily. The darkness is not dispelled or illuminated. It remains vast, untamed, void. But he somehow encompasses it. It becomes the darkness of God. It is now possible to enter the darkness and trust God to wrest from it meaning, coherence, resurrection.

Sooner or later something happens that changes the shape of our world. And then we, like disciples who loved Jesus, come completely undone. Suddenly we are faced with the awful vulnerability of our humanity. This vulnerability to suffering and different kinds of emotional endings—moving away, the loss of a job, the ending of a friend-ship you thought would last forever—as well as death itself, is some-thing that we try to control at the very least, and we often seek to deny it outright.

Sometimes it is a death that undoes us. A spouse dies; there is a tragic accident, and a friend dies; a child is diagnosed with leukemia and dies—despite everyone's fervent prayers; an elderly parent passes on, and while others say the death is a blessing, we are completely undone.

Sometimes it is not literally a death, but it feels like a death—a divorce looms, a son or daughter loses their way, a church conflict makes a sanctuary no longer safe, a chronic illness is diagnosed, a friend betrays us or we lose a job that was not simply a livelihood but part of our identity and calling. Or it might be the recognition of our own sinfulness, a deeper understanding that we are not the person that others believe we are or that we thought we were.

⤳ Entering the Darkness

Remember a place of suffering in your own life, in the life of someone you know or in the life of the world. Let your-self experience its weight and heaviness. How did things unravel and become so difficult? List words you associate with this sorrow and death. See if there is an image or picture that expresses what might be beyond words, then draw or describe this picture. Perhaps there are colors or shapes that loom around this place of suffering.

A friend whose baby died just hours after his birth wrote in her own journal to comfort herself while she was still in the chaos of her own grief. Describing herself as "an animal raging," she explains:

I write to turn my animal-like grunts into speech. . . . I need to hold this experience open in the palm of my hand and examine it, as one might an exotic yet terrifying bug that has just landed on my arm. The whole situation makes no sense to me. As adults we want to fix situations. We want answers. But it is just this desire to fix that makes me feel people are not really receptive to my problem, the mess of it, the inexplicability of it. Knowing that people are uncomfortable with the unknown, I have become private and territorial with my grief. I guard my feelings. I will not let others come in and give me answers, especially if they don't take the time, due to discomfort, to enter into my questions.

She found that the most hospitable and welcome place for her grief was at the cross of Jesus Christ. "To live at the foot of the cross in daily life means to live in the mess of life without trying to evade it."

From the earliest times, Christians followed Jesus Christ along the Way of the Cross in prayer, not just as a sign of love and devotion to Jesus but also to bring meaning to the sorrows in their own lives. The Way of the Cross was a personal pilgrimage to Jerusalem, retracing the way of Jesus' last hours as he walked to Calvary, carried the cross, died on the cross and was buried in the tomb. It is a prayer journey that leads us into an experience of Emmanuel, God with us, even in our suffering. Throughout history, many who wanted to walk the Way of the Cross were unable to go to Jerusalem because of their poverty or physical infirmities. During the thirteenth century, churches began providing depictions of scenes from the Way of the Cross, usually through paintings or carvings placed along the walls of a church. The stopping places along the way were called the Stations of the Cross. Over time, there came to be fourteen stations, some of them reflecting biblical scenes and others depicting a human understanding of Jesus' suffering. The Stations of the Cross are not just about what happened on that day in history; they are meant to show the depth of Jesus' suffering love and to invite our prayerful response. They are a pilgrimage pathway not around the pain of Christ or our own human pain but through it.

Another way of making this pilgrimage of prayer is to immerse ourselves in the biblical story of Christ's passion, beginning with Jesus' prayer in the garden of Gethsemane. The Gospel stories all invite us to slow down when we come to the suffering and death of Jesus, letting us know that this is a crucial part of Jesus' own story, just as crucial for us to walk with him as it was for the first disciples.

⤳ Walking the Way of the Cross

Carry with you the sorrow of your own life as you accept Jesus' invitation to make this painful journey with him to his death. Choose one of the Gospel accounts, and identify individual scenes along the way to the cross. Try to see what Jesus saw along the way, feel what he might have felt, touch what he touched, smell what he smelled and taste what he tasted. You might try writing a prayer at each of these biblical stops along the way, or drawing a picture, either abstract or realistic. (You might find Megan McKenna's book to be a helpful resource.) After you have completed your journey, stop once more to look back on your walk. How does being with Jesus in his suffering and pain affect your own sorrow? Which station seemed most moving or meaningful, troubling or comforting? Why? You might also choose to take a virtual walk along the Stations of the Cross, praying as directed along the way. One

helpful website (among many) is www.creighton.edu/
CollaborativeMinistry/Stations.html.

When the women arrived at the tomb of Jesus Christ, the most
they hoped for was to put spices on Jesus' dead body. They must have
wondered how they would even perform this simple act of love without having the strength to roll away the stone. But a power greater
than theirs had already come to the tomb. God had raised Jesus from
the dead! Still, the first response of the women was not joy and victory but astonishment and fear. This was so beyond understanding
that they clung to what they knew before. Ronald Rolheiser captures
Mary's reluctance to let go of the Jesus she knew and loved before his
crucifixion:

I never suspected
    Resurrection
        and to be so painful
to leave me weeping
With joy
        to have met you, alive and smiling, outside an empty
    tomb
With regret
not because I've lost you
but because I've lost you in how I had you—
        in understandable, touchable, kissable, clingable
            flesh
        not as fully Lord, but as graspably human.

I want to cling, despite your protest
    cling to your body
cling to your and my clingable humanity
cling to what we had, our past.

But I know that . . . if I cling
you cannot ascend and
I will be left clinging to your former self
. . . unable to receive your present spirit.

The inability of the disciples to recognize Jesus, not just once but over and over, tells us that Jesus himself was changed by the resurrection. Something about Jesus was truly transformed when God raised him from the dead. Yes, this is Jesus—but this Jesus is also new, unexpected and even unrecognizable if you are simply looking for the pre-crucifixion Jesus. His journey through death to the tomb and to resurrection transformed him. Nevertheless, through their grief and doubt, their fear and sadness, the disciples did recognize the presence of the risen Christ in the context of their own lives.

For Mary, that recognition came when Jesus spoke her name. For the two on the road to Emmaus, it was in the breaking of bread that their eyes were opened and they saw him. For the disciples huddled in fear behind a locked door, it was in realizing that Jesus was truly human and not a ghost that they knew the resurrection of his body was real. For Thomas, just seeing the holes in Jesus' hands made him cry out, "My Lord and my God!" (John 20:28). Remembering brings recognition to the fishing disciples who saw their empty nets fill up, and the disciple who knew Jesus best shouted out, "It is the Lord!" (John 21:7).

➤ Recognizing the Risen Jesus Christ

Record in your journal where you have seen the risen Christ in the context of your own life, especially during times of grief or sorrow, doubt or despair, fear or anxiety, or times

when it might have been difficult to recognize him. Was it
a word, a touch, a voice that you heard or a confirmation of
what you knew, a sense of peace, an insight, a way forward
or a rest? What was this presence like, and how might it
speak to whatever is troubling you today?

It is always a temptation to hurry the grief-stricken along into the
victory of the resurrection without acknowledging the pain and darkness, the void and emptiness that is Holy Saturday, the entombment
that is also necessary for the journey. We hesitate to explore with others the extremities of their suffering, yet it is in this place where God's
best work is being done. A widowed friend observed that grief in suffering and death is inevitable. The loss of her spouse was, she said,
"like being run over by a truck. I felt flattened and lifeless." But for her,
mourning was a choice to be fully alive to what was happening in her,
to cry out to God loudly and name all the losses that she faced each day.
Surprisingly to her it was in this place of mourning that signs of hope
and new life began to appear. She was able to see through her tears the
possibility of life in Christ reshaped now by her own sorrow.

When we feel all torn apart and entombed by the reality of loss and
death, it is then that God's good (though hidden) work is being accom-
plished. But the transformation that takes place after a time of suffering and death will not return the person to who they were before, but
into someone who is transformed by the experience of suffering. Like
the disciples who followed Jesus, we may be tempted to cling to what
we knew rather than receive the new life that Jesus offers to us in his
death and resurrection. But Christ's hope is that we will let go and
trust God who gave life to give again in an even deeper way.

Sometimes when I listen to people who have gone through suffering and pain, and who have lived it out as a journey through death to

life, my eyes are opened and I recognize the Spirit of Christ alive in them. This new life might appear as a courageous spirit, a compassion for the suffering of others or a gift of insight. Another might have a more mature faith or a greater willingness to risk, or a clearer understanding of the injustices that others experience in their lives. Like the disciples who saw Jesus after the resurrection, I am often surprised and astonished.

The transformative journey of Jesus from the cross to the tomb to resurrection life is the heartbeat and hope of our own Christian faith life. It is Jesus' own journey through death, burial and resurrection that gives us the pattern and pathway through our sufferings and deaths— and finally through death itself to resurrection. But as Richard Rohr says, we Christians have been "worshiping Jesus' journey instead of *doing* his journey. The first feels very religious, the second feels just human and not glorious at all." The irony is that it is only in fully living and being with our own suffering and death that we experience in our own lives the movement from "mourning into dancing" (Psalm 30:11).

The rhythm of redeeming grace might be slow in what feels like a tomb or an actual experience of death, but the rhythm continues. Our former understandings are deconstructed, and new hopes are born out of the ashes of the past. There are many ways we can avoid taking up this cross and following Christ. Taking up our cross in suffering is a messy, painful task, but so it was for Jesus. Our perspective might be deconstructed and our priorities altered as we choose to live outside our comfort zone. But it is the way of the cross that is ultimately the way of life and not death.

When we experience our own suffering we seek out people who are willing to walk with us through the valley of the shadow of death. Often they will be people whose own walk to the other side of suffering makes them uniquely able to accompany others. They will encourage us to ask the hard and deep questions, even if there are no easy or convenient answers. These are questions that even Jesus himself asked as he was dying on the cross. He cried out, "My God, my God, why have you forsaken me?" (Matthew 27:46). These are the friends who will believe for us when we cannot believe. These are the friends who will hold on to the resurrection when death is the only reality we can perceive with our limited vision and understanding.

⤳ Naming My Community

List in your journal those people with whom you could be honest and real during a time of suffering and death. Who will let you ask the hard and deep questions that might arise? Who will be able to hold the light of hope for you when your own light is dimmed by suffering? This community may be a community of one or two or three, but each of us needs to know where we will turn when the darkness closes in. What gift does each of these people bring to your community? If you are unable to name anyone, begin to look around you and see whom God might have placed in your life for this purpose. What might it mean to begin a relationship with this friend or spiritual director, a pastor or mentor?

Despite all of the strategies and analyses and plans we make, suffering happens in human life. We don't truly know for certain what lies ahead for us. But we know that we have a friend in Jesus, who has walked where we walk, who has suffered where we have suffered, whom God raised from the dead, and whose Spirit is living among us and in us.

12

DISCOVERING LIFE

Writing for Healing

>︵︵<

Desperate to find a way to stop drinking, poet and memoir writer Mary Karr admitted that she had tried "everything *but* prayer." So when somebody suggested to her that she begin her day by kneeling and asking God to help her not pick up that cocktail and then kneel at night once more to say thanks, Karr protested, "But I don't even believe in God." Her friend responded that Karr wouldn't be doing it for God, but for her own survival. Having tried everything else, Karr listened to her friend and found a path to sobriety—and to God. As she continued in her life of prayer, a fellow poet suggested that she begin her day by simply saying thank you. Saying this prayer changed something not in her world but in the way she saw herself and the world around her.

> I started to follow his advice by mouthing rote thank-yous to the air, and right off, I discovered something. There was an entire aspect to my life that I had been blind to—the small, good thing that came in abundance. A friend had once told me regarding his own faith, "I've memorized the bad news." . . . Having all

my life disdained as nonsense any spiritual or religious practice, I eventually realized that I'd always believed in a magical force for evil. . . . I interpreted the world through my own grief or self-absorbed fear.

Even for us who say we believe in a loving God, it is easy to convince ourselves that it is our own sin and evil, as well as the sin and evil around us, that is the more realistic worldview. Knowing at the core of our being that God's love for us is the single, constant reality of our life can sometimes seem difficult to comprehend. We all bear wounds that might come from violence, neglect or silence; wounds from the absence or death of a parent, an illness suffered by ourselves or someone close to us, an injury inflicted on us, or one that we inflicted on someone close to us. Even human love that is well intended can be wounding.

Naming the wounds of the past or present in our journal can help us to heal hurts rather than hold on to them. The journal can be a safe place to say it all, name it all and leave it all—perhaps even returning to our lives with a new understanding as our listening continues in our writing and our living. Rather than overcoming or forgetting our wounds, we may find a way through them. As we begin to write about what happened and the pain we feel, we may find that our wounds, as real as they are, do not define us. Such self-transcendence is always a gift of God, but our journals can become a place to receive that gift of love and compassion.

➳ Heart Wounds and Scars

Begin by drawing a large heart, and then mark your wounds on it. Some are obvious: your parents' divorce or your brother's death or a friend's suicide. But others are more subtle: not making it onto the baseball team, your mother's passive-aggressive behavior toward you, a friend's betrayal. Some of these might be scars from the past; still others might be raw, unhealed wounds. Choose one of these wounds, and tell what happened and how you see the wound or scar and its effect on your life. Notice the places where there has been movement or where you feel stuck. Keep a reminder of God's unconditional love nearby as you write, whether a song, a picture, a card from a dear friend or a few flowers in a vase. If you begin to feel overwhelmed, stop writing and return to it another day.

If we have been very deeply wounded, it may be difficult for us to trust in God. It may be hard for us to believe that God desires us and longs to hold us close. When the Israelites were in exile, wounded and feeling forgotten, the prophet Isaiah brought them these words of comfort: "The LORD comforts his people / and will have compassion on his afflicted ones" (Isaiah 49:13 NIV). But Zion—or you or I—says, "The LORD has forsaken me, / the Lord has forgotten me" (v. 14). Then God responds, "Can a mother forget the baby at her breast / and have no compassion on the child she has borne? / Though she may forget, / I will not forget you! / See, I have engraved you on the palms of my hands" (vv. 15-16). This God, who does not forget even when human love fails, is always ready and able to love and heal us. Brennan Manning, an author who has known his share of suffering and recovery, says it this way: "You must be convinced of this, trust it and never forget to remember. Everything else will pass away, but the love of Christ is the same yesterday, today and forever. Faith will become vision, hope will become possession, but the love of Jesus Christ that is stronger than death endures forever. In the end, it is the one thing you can hang onto."

Healing from wounds is a long, messy process of letting go of those things that do not belong to us and letting God continue to form his image within us, literally enlarging our own capacity to hold God's Spirit. Listen to an abuse survivor as she describes what it meant for her to embrace God's love for her:

> This idea that God loved me upset all my false beliefs. . . . I have to accept what I now believe to be true: I am good because God created me. At first this idea so disoriented me that I felt like I was walking on the ceiling of an upside-down room. But I came to believe in that goodness despite all the evil that had been done to me. . . . All of this requires discipline. I must fight to defeat the devils that plague me, the voices that tell me over and over again that I am worth nothing, that life must be full of sadness and that I was born to suffer.

Our ability to trust in God's love for us at those painful places in our lives can be both helped and hindered by the pictures of God that we carry with us. The way we name God tells a story not only about our understanding of God but about how we see ourselves in relationship to God. If we name Jesus as our shepherd, then we will see ourselves as sheep in his pasture. If we name God as our lover, then we will be named in that relationship as the beloved.

In one of the classes I teach, I give the students a list of fifteen names that are taken from the biblical psalms. The names include Jehovah and Father, King and Friend, Mother, Rock, Provider, Lover, Creator and Shepherd. Then I ask them to choose a name for God that they are most comfortable with and one that they are least comfortable with. Inevitably students are surprised to find that the names they are least comfortable with are cherished by others as a way of picturing their relationship with God. As a teacher, I am always surprised at how few names most of us actually have for God and how tenaciously we cling to our personal picture of God. This is true even though any human picture is only the barest sort of metaphor for a God who transcends all we know in the created world.

⟶ *Naming God*

Remember a name for God that has been especially important in your faith life. It might be one of the names I mentioned earlier or some other name that has been part of your own prayer. Write this name in your journal, and tell the story of how God has met you in this name. How has saying this name aloud named you as son or daughter, disciple or beloved? How do you see through this metaphorical picture to the true God? Take a few moments to thank God for the gift of this name and for the relationship that has grown out of the naming. Now ask yourself if there might be a new name for God emerging in your prayer or as you journal. Write this name in your journal as well as any Scriptures or personal experiences that it recalls for you. How might God be naming you in a new way through this picture?

I experienced such a new way of God naming me during a retreat. As he had with his disciples, Jesus insisted that he no longer wanted to call me servant but friend. As a child I would often try to please God while at the same time constantly feeling that I was unworthy of being God's child. While such an attitude might be part of a servant's or slave's role, it seemed inappropriate for a friendship with Jesus. Being with Jesus as a friend is with a friend would mean valuing myself in a new way. I wondered what it might mean to find a sense of mutual enjoyment rather than only personal obligation in my life with God.

Sometimes a distorted and untrue image of God as a harsh judge or a rigid enforcer grows in a childhood atmosphere of fear or control and continues to wound a person for life. For some, the church only confirms what their difficult life experience has taught them:

> Being abused had taught me that I was nothing, an object to be used. . . . The only way I knew I was alive was to feel pain. . . . This was my mantra: Life is pain, and anyone who tells you different is lying. What the church had taught me only reinforced that belief. In church I learned about giving yourself, about denying yourself in order to serve. . . . I learned that to be like Christ I had to be willing to give up my life. Being a Christian, I believed, meant suffering. The pick-up-your-cross-and-follow-me command carried a lot of weight. To me, the Golden Rule— love your neighbor as yourself—meant loving your neighbor at the expense of yourself.

But this did not seem to fit with what this abuse survivor knew about Jesus. Instead of letting people suffer, Jesus healed people. Instead of ignoring the pain around him, Jesus not only brought healing, he entered into that pain himself. When the hemorrhaging woman reached out to touch Jesus as he walked through the crowd, he not only healed her wounds but he commended her for her boldness. With the words "Your faith has made you well," Jesus reached across the barrier between the clean and the unclean and claimed the woman's own longing to be healed as part of his own ministry of healing (see Luke 8:40-48). Seeing Jesus and understanding him to be God's human face made abuse survivor Melanie Jansen reconsider her assumptions about living a life of faith. Finally she admitted, "Perhaps, I reasoned, life doesn't mean just suffering after all. Maybe, and this was a big maybe for me, I could be healed."

⟫⟫ Embodied Biblical Prayer

Read Luke 13:10-16 (aloud if possible) while bending over
as the woman in the story is bent over. Allow yourself to
feel whatever it is that cripples you and makes you bent
over. Stay in this position long enough to really feel its effect. What do you notice about being physically and emo-
tionally bent over? Now read the passage a second time
(again reading aloud). Begin in the same bent-over position, but allow yourself to feel Jesus physically setting you
free from this crippling condition. What do you notice in
yourself as you stand up tall and straight?

Letting go of an outworn behavior, a false belief or an attitude that
no longer fits our present reality may be necessary for us to grow and
change. While the experience of pain can paralyze us, wounds that are
named and given voice in a journal or in talking with a friend or in a
support group can become a courageous pathway into a new reality.
Abuse survivor Jansen ends her last meditation with these words:

Putting my hope in God is to believe, to trust that I will find the
courage to put one foot in front of another. I cannot change the
past, and I don't have a great deal of control over the future. I
was not saved from being abused, nor am I being miraculously
healed from it. But right now, in this moment, I can choose to
move. And every step that I take brings me closer to the other
side of the desert.

After the resurrection, Jesus Christ showed the nail marks in his
hands to Thomas and the other disciples. When Thomas saw the nail
marks, he knew this was the crucified Jesus. But when he saw that
the wounds were *transfigured* in Christ's resurrection, he cried out,

"My Lord and my God!" (John 20:28). It was only then that he knew what the prophet Isaiah spoke about—"by his wounds we are healed" (Isaiah 53:5 NIV). So, too, it is only when we let God transfigure our wounds that they can become healing for others and ourselves. This does not mean that our wounds disappear, any more than this was true of Jesus after his resurrection, or that it makes right the wrongs of the past. It does mean that our wounds can provide hospitality to others because the wounds of the past no longer define us. Our wounds have been transfigured by Christ's own healing power.

Recheck Your Personal Compass

Turn back to your personal compass from the journaling exercise in chapter nine. Spend some time facing in the westward direction again. What or who needs to be released? What old beliefs or attitudes or maps do you need to let go of? Where is deep healing needed? Look in the eastward direction, and ask, what is calling you forward? Where is the new beginning or possibility that you see there? What will you need to let go of to move in this direction?

If we are able to name our wounds and grieve them, we might be surprised to find that even a painful past can bless us and others. Recently someone described her leadership role in a large Christian organization as providing ballast to right the organization when things go wrong. "I do that as I listen and pray with others and share a few words of hope. But I think it feels real to people because I've not only experienced real suffering, I've experienced real redemption through Christ." In her leadership role, she is allowing her painful past to bless others going through pain in the present.

A wife whose husband died of AIDS finds herself returning to the AIDS clinic to provide comfort. A breast cancer survivor listens and responds on her blog to those in chemotherapy. Someone who attempted suicide works the midnight shift on the suicide prevention hotline. A recovering addict speaks words of tough love as a sponsor of another addict who is struggling to stop using. Each of them is letting a painful past bless themselves and others.

Whether we are experiencing the pain of abuse or the struggle with an addiction, the suffering of serious illness or the losses that come as we age, such difficulties can seem terminal to us, a sort of death in life. But when we move through the pain and share it in our journal and with God, we may find ourselves moving to life in the midst of death. This healing comes not because we have overcome our hurts and losses but because we have incorporated this pain into our very being, especially in those places that may never be cured but can always be healed. Such a healing does not lift us above our human vulnerability but blesses it with God's presence and the light of Christ. Here we find ourselves living out of a deeper, more profound vulnerability that brings hope not just for ourselves but for the suffering world around us as well. Robert Collen writes of this experience:

> Look! It is winter, and you have come
> alone to this clearing in the wood,
> a familiar place you have never
> seen before. Do not hurry to leave,
> but when at last you turn away,
> remember this, if you remember nothing else,
> you are no longer who you were.

13

SEEING THE HOLY
IN THE ORDINARY

Noticing God in the Everyday

⊱⊰

W hen my now grown children were little, I began saying the following blessing over them when they went to bed:

May the love of God watch over you.
May the peace of Christ fill your heart.
May the presence of the Holy Spirit fill your sleep,
    and speak in your dreams.

It wasn't long before my daughter, ever the one to notice who was being left out, said, "It doesn't seem fair, Mommy, that all of us get blessed but you don't." I thought about it and had to agree with her. If ever there was someone that needed this particular blessing, it was this harried mother of three children. From then on, after I blessed my children, they said the same blessing over me.

To bless is to see the good that God sees. If Jesus is to be followed and obeyed, this means blessing our friends and our family, the lost and the least, even our enemies, both near and far, ones whose names we know and those who are nameless individuals within a hated people group. To bless means to be a seeker after good and to restore to our spirits a sense of wonder, perhaps even awe.

All spiritual practice, including journaling, is meant to tune our awareness, just as you might tune a stringed instrument, so that we can hear the true note of God's grace playing through the sometimes discordant chords around us and in us. And then it means choosing to let this graced note bless us and others. If we miss the blessing in us and around us, we will never be able to see the holy in the ordinary. At least in my own life, choosing to bless rather than curse has not always been such an obvious choice.

When my youngest son was five years old, he broke one of our living-room lamps—and shattered me as well. It was not really about the lamp, but the broken lamp was a symbol of my sense of failure as a mother. Holding that broken lamp in my hands, I confessed to a dear friend and to God what a dismal mess I'd made of meeting my third child's needs. The other two children could be difficult at times, but in some fundamental way, I knew them. They were truly bone of my bone and flesh of my flesh. But this child seemed to have been dropped into our family like an alien from some distant planet. As the third child, I expected him simply to come along with the others in everything, but he refused. From the time that he could speak, he barely tolerated—and later outright refused—any spontaneous physical affection. Spur-of-the-moment outings to the park or shopping or to a friend's house delighted my older two children but held no appeal for the third and sometimes seemed a bit frightening to him. I could not find the pathway into this child's heart.

What I realized in that time of confession was that I did not know my youngest son. I had valiantly set out mothering him in the same way I had the older two, without actually getting to know him. Now I had to start all over with my parenting. This time I needed to actually see him as an individual rather than as someone who could be molded into a child resembling his older siblings or myself.

So I began watching and listening to my own child. I realized that he himself was a watcher first rather than a doer. While my other children learned by trial and error, he learned by watching until he understood, and only then did he try things in a tentative, careful way. When something didn't make sense to him, it was more difficult. A two-wheeled bicycle was difficult for him to learn because it meant believing that those two tires could hold a child, let alone an adult. And he could not simply get on and do it. I tried to show him how by running alongside him and then letting go, but that first fall was all he needed to convince him to wheel the bike back into the garage. He also liked more control than the other two children. It wasn't that he did not like to go to the park or go shopping with me. But he wanted to know where we would stop and how long we would stay there and when we would have a snack. Clearly surprises were not fun for him.

There was more of him that I had been missing. He had a quirky, offbeat sense of humor that my husband had plugged into long before I had. He was bright and creative in his own way—though as introverted as I was extroverted. I saw, too, that he was thoughtful about issues large and small, hearing and watching everything and mulling it over within himself. It took him a while to form an opinion, but once formed, he held to his beliefs strongly, some might say stubbornly. This could also make him disciplined in understanding and practice. In his quiet, watching, listening way, he missed little that was going on around him. When he saw someone that was troubled or needed help, he responded with a surprising (to me) kindness.

As I began to follow him rather than expecting him to follow me, I fell in love again with my own son. If I asked permission, I was even able to hug him and tell him how remarkable he truly was (and is).

Nothing changed about my youngest son as I watched him. What changed was my own perception of him and who he was. I had missed the holy in the ordinary in my own child. What else had I missed while I was busy unthinkingly and unknowingly following my own way?

⤳ Taking a Second Look

> Choose a person who is close to you, someone whom you might take for granted. Take a second or third look at this person. Try using a journalistic stance, setting yourself apart from this person and observing what is happening around and in him or her. Watch how others who know her interact with her. Interview these other people to get an impression of how they see him. Record what you learned and any surprises that you found by watching this person. Did anything change in your own way of seeing him? How might that shift your perspective or change your way of interacting with her?

The simplest shift in perspective can open up a whole new way of seeing. Recently a friend recounted all of the frustrations she felt during a visit from a younger sister who is very different from her. But as she continued to describe the details of all her sister's annoying habits, a smile began to form where there had been a frown of disgust. The smile turned into a chuckle, which turned into laughter. Suddenly she was aware of how funny it was when their two very different personalities collided together in her house. She remembered how everyone in her family had laughed together at the crazy differences between the two sisters. Just retelling it and seeing it all for a second time broke the tension that she felt about her sister and gave her hope.

Poet Elizabeth Barrett Browning wrote,

Earth's crammed with heaven
And every bush afire with God.
But only he who sees takes off his shoes
the rest sit round and pluck blackberries.

I'll be the first to say that there is nothing wrong with eating black-berries. Still, what makes an ordinary moment a moment of beauty and holiness is the presence and perception that we bring to it. This way of seeing the holy in the ordinary is not automatically ours because we say we believe or because we go to church or even because we pray or journal. But your journal can be the window you choose to not only see into your life, but to see through it into the sacredness of each day, of every person. It is a daily choice to live as a seeker after truth and beauty and kindness rather than as a bitter cynic. God does not merely tolerate our eccentricities, but he loves and delights in us—even to the extent of counting the hairs on our head. God himself chose to love us in all of the everydayness of who we are. If God continues to love us and hope for the best in us, can we do any less?

➳ Taking a Contemplative Prayer Walk

Begin by praying to be available to God's presence as you take a walk through your own neighborhood, whether it is a city street, a suburban cul-de-sac, a rural field or the main street of the small town where you live. If you are carrying a particular concern or question, write it down in your journal, close the journal and leave it behind. Go for a walk alone, and deliberately slow down your pace. Stay alert to the outside world rather than mulling over things in your head. Use your eyes to take in things both close-up and at a distance. Pay attention to shapes, colors

and textures. Notice the relationship of things to one another. What attracts your attention? Spend some time exploring this. Really listen to sounds around you as well as
sounds inside you. Use touch to become aware of different
textures; allow yourself to feel, both physically and emo-
tionally. Listen for anything God might be trying to say
through your environment and surroundings. As you end
your walk, you may want to take something with you—a
stone or a twig or a flower—as a reminder of what you
experienced. In your journal, report what you saw. Look
again at the concerns or questions you left behind, and see
if there has been any change in your understanding or any
shift in your perspective.

A man who was a schoolteacher for more than twenty years tells
a story of finding an unexpected gift. Every Christmas the teacher
received gifts from his students. After several years, he could guess
what was inside each wrapped package just from the shape of the box.
Each year he put the long, thin boxes that held handkerchiefs on the
top shelf of his closet. When he needed a handkerchief, he would pull
down one of the boxes and take one out. One day he pulled down the
next handkerchief box, opened it and found inside an antique watch.
"What a surprise," said the man. "All this time I had an antique wrist-
watch and never knew it!"

Like this teacher, we make assumptions about people and places in
our lives by looking at the size and shape of the box and guessing what
is inside. Then we file what we think we know in the back closet of
our lives for later use. But what if we are as wrong as the teacher was
about what is inside the long, thin box? What if there is something
inside that is more valuable than what it appears from the outside, and

we have just never bothered to open it up and look?

It is easy for us to get attached to the boxes that our own lives and the lives of those around us are lived in, rather than to see the beauty that is there on the inside. Our common practice is to define ourselves and others by what we do—the stay-at-home mom, the working mom, the single parent, the church member, the runner, the caretaker of an elderly parent, the CEO, the housekeeper, the truck driver. Or we attach ourselves to a certain identity we have chosen or were given—the single woman, the child of an alcoholic, the Volvo owner, the suburbanite, the preacher's kid, the youngest child, the oldest child or the child stuck in the middle. But these are all just boxes that we live in, boxes that really give only the broadest of hints about what is inside.

Still, we cling to the boxes to understand ourselves and others. When the boxes are organized and labeled, or even just stuffed in the back of the closet, then our lives are neat and presentable. But God is forever opening up all of the boxes, looking inside and finding the valuables we missed in our haste to organize or hide our own messiness.

As you look back on all of the journaling we've done together, I hope you can see that God was the audience to your writing, which often felt like praying. I hope that you have caught a glimpse of how hard God has laughed at the funny parts and how deeply grieved he has been for all of the suffering, then and now. I hope you have seen how delighted God is with the risks you took to come closer to his love in your life and with the times you embodied his love in your life with others. Sometimes it may have felt like a messy business. Boxes that you might have stacked neatly or at the very least pushed to the back of your life were thrown open, their contents spilled out on the journal page. But until the boxes are opened, it is difficult to see what is inside and what truly matters.

↬ What I Found Inside

Take a look back at the journal writing you've done. As you look at the boxes that you opened in your journal, where was the antique watch that was there all along but you never knew it? Recall how astonished you were by the beauty that was hidden inside a seemingly predictable box. This time don't box it up again and store it away in the back of your personal closet. How will you claim this extraordinary gift as your own and honor it in your everyday life? Write in your journal about the ways you will wear this valuable gift in your everyday life.

Seeing the holy in the ordinary, the sacredness in the everyday, is about leaning into the mystery at the center of human life, not counting up successes and accomplishments. It is about seeing and following the love and compassion that God has already placed in us and in the world. If we understand and believe that God can be experienced through all things—sorrow and joy, struggle and victory, conflict and peace, mountain, sea and sky; if we understand and believe that it is safe for us to be honest about how it is with us; if we understand, believe or even want to believe that God is able to transform us, we will find ourselves in God's presence, no matter where we are in our lives. Our journals will not then simply repeat our life circumstances but will reveal God's glory. We will find that the ordinary is not ordinary at all but is shot through with the presence of the Holy One. As poet and priest Gerard Manley Hopkins saw:

The world is charged with the grandeur of God.
It will flame out, like shining from shook foil.
It gathers to greatness like ooze of oil
Crushed.

During the last months of my mother's life, as lung cancer crept up to her brain and then out to other parts of her body, she picked up a book with the peculiar title *Cancer Has Its Privileges* at her doctor's office. She showed me the book, and the title shocked us both. But the title proved prophetic as through her own life, cancer's unexpected privileges began to appear. Because the lung cancer was able to be treated with palliative chemotherapy, the doctors assured us that brain cancer in her elderly body would not be painful because there was room in the cranial cavity for her brain to expand. For a few brief months, the cancer even transformed my mother's chronic disappointment with life into an attitude of blessed acceptance.

After she began her cancer treatments, my mother refused to return to the church that she had helped to found and had attended all her life. Perhaps she did not trust that an attitude of blessed acceptance would find a home there. For my mother, church was a place where everyone arrived in their predictable boxes. But the cancer made her self-conscious about not being her usual church-member self. How could she explain the illness that narrowed her already narrow face? What might people say to her or about her? And what if someone looked longer than she was comfortable with at the wig she wore to cover her baldness? Surely that would be embarrassing.

Though she refused to go to church, my mother looked forward to her weekly treatments at the oncology clinic, finding there a place of acceptance and welcome. She was like an elderly oncological poster child for the palliative treatments she received, and her doctor was invariably delighted with her continued ability to care for herself in assisted living. The nurses in the oncology clinic were warm and compassionate, offering juice and crackers during treatments. The colorful assortment of hats and scarves decorating the bathroom wall were available for the taking to cover up the inevitable hair loss the cancer treatments caused. Patients talked together freely about their cancer, their times of treatments, their physical and emotional frustrations and their fatigue.

My mother dressed for those treatments at the oncology clinic with the same care she had once dressed for church. "What do you think?" she asked. "Would it be better to wear the gray sweater with the pearl earrings, or the red blouse with the small silver hoops?" Now I realize that she found her community for this final passing in the oncology clinic, where she was treated as an honored guest. It was there that she received a final blessing, a way through into the arms of God.

Sometimes we fool ourselves into believing that we can only experience the holy in the guise of whatever a "perfect" experience might be for us—a spiritual high in a worship service, a vista from the top of a mountain or a retreat in a remote monastery. But what if it is waiting all the time for us in the most mundane and even most dreaded parts of human life? Will we be able to dress for the occasion and honor it as my mother did? Or will we be so busy staring off in the distance and waiting for God to appear that we miss the holy presence in the everyday?

14

FACING RESISTANCE

Finding the Pathway Home

>⌒⌒⌒⌒<

Every year my family celebrates a Seder service and meal together around the long wooden table in my dining room. As the mother of the household, it is my responsibility to begin the Seder by lighting the candles and symbolically pulling in the candle's light to me and sending the light out to all who are gathered. With that inner light, we remember together. We remember together the slavery of the Hebrew people and their miraculous journey to freedom. The Haggadah is the retelling of the story that surrounds this meal of remembrance. The retelling begins with questions asked by the youngest at the table, those who have the least experience with the journey from slavery to freedom. The questions are, "Why is this night different from all other nights?" and, "Why do we eat these special foods and sit in this special way?" Answering the questions reminds us of the time when the people of Israel were slaves in Egypt and their lives were bitter and difficult. They remind us of the night of the hurried journey out of Egypt and when the Hebrews fled through the Red Sea on dry land.

But one Haggadah (there are many retellings of this story) ends with a final question that we all still need to answer in our own lives—"How does the journey to freedom continue?" The first person to respond to this question says, "Following fire and cloud, we stumble, shivering with cold and fear. Some will always cry out for Egypt, longing to return to the known." Then the same question is asked once more: "How does the journey to freedom continue?" Another person says, "Risking together what we never imagined possible on our own, we keep walking. The sea rises to our nostrils. Then, with a breath, the waters part." The question is asked a third time, and someone else responds, "We build fragile shelters and watch as they sway in the wind. Aching for a song, our throats are parched. The water is too bitter to drink. Even manna sometimes tastes like sand." When the question is asked a fourth time, all say together, "But ours is a holy journey. We falter, but we do not turn back. Embracing the challenge of tradition, we clear new paths to the future. Ours is a holy journey, a journey towards new life."

Ours, too, is a holy journey toward new life. My hope is that your journal is a retelling of a journey toward God. Like the children of Israel, you may have come through honest complaint and longing, adversity and suffering. Perhaps you have found yourself filled with wonder, gratitude and awe as you see the power of God at work in your life. My prayer is that this journey has been a journey toward freedom for you, as it was for those earlier travelers; that you have found through journaling as a spiritual practice the freedom to follow Jesus Christ toward new life and living out of God's love at the heart of your life experience. Rereading your journal is a way of remembering that even through times of uncertainty and transition, God is leading you toward a new land.

⤳ Remembering Our Journey

Look back on everything you have written since you began the journaling exercises in this book. Using a highlighter (or several different colors of highlighters), mark places where themes recurred in your own life with God. Mark as well any "aha" insights that moved you forward toward God or reflections that let you rest in God. After you have reread your journal, ask, what remains to be heard or said or understood? Is there a question that needs to be asked or an issue to be explored or understood? If you see something that remains unfinished, stay with it and write about it in your journal.

Taking the time to see patterns, to listen to themes, to remember repeated thoughts or images is all part of honoring where the journal has taken you and where it leads in your own journey. Your journal is a way of celebrating the goodness of the Lord, who gives us a pathway through even difficult times and encourages us to be all we were created to be and do, say and live.

⤳ Remembering with God

Look back once more over everything that you have written since you began journaling with this book. Suspending any judgment, listen to what you have said, where you have been, your struggles, your hopes, your joys along the way. Write a prayer as a response to God about everything you have seen and heard and understood, even if some of what you see is troubling or painful or puzzling. Perhaps your prayer will be one of supplication or conviction, gratitude or adoration, lament or joy. Wherever you are on your journey, God will receive this prayer with love.

I am often impatient with myself when an old familiar problem or frustration or anxiety reappears in my journal. Yet these companions, too, are a part of my journey home. Allow yourself to feel some grace instead of frustration about struggling with the same questions and problems. In listening to people talk about their faith journey, I often say that we are a bit like the old phonograph records with a scratch at a certain place on the record. Each time the needle hits the scratch, there is the same sound or distortion; but each time, the needle is a bit closer to the center. So, too, in our own lives we find that the scratches remain, but each time the needle of our own life goes over the scratch, we are a little closer to the center, to the truth of the matter. Thomas Merton noticed a similar phenomenon in his own life and writing:

> Keeping a journal has taught me that there is not so much new in your life as you sometimes think. When you reread your journal, you find out that your latest discovery is something you already found out about five years ago. Still it is true that one penetrates deeper and deeper into the same ideas and the same experiences.

Your journal is also a record of the ways you might have changed, grown, rethought a destructive path and chosen a new way. Sometimes a difficult relationship finds a new place of reconciliation, or we understand a better way to approach someone who seemed to be a threat to us. Observing this as you reread your journal should be cause for celebration and gratitude.

⤙ Bringing It Forward

When you find something in your own journal that catches your attention or is an interesting insight, write it down

and add some thoughts that show how this has been re-
inforced, changed or shown to be false. For example,
write "On Monday, February 13, I wrote in my journal
_____. Today I feel _____.

Sometimes as we reread our journals, we recognize that there is
unfinished business that needs to be taken care of. Recently I reread
in my own journal an entry about the unexpected support I received
from my friend Carol during a particular time when I felt alone and
anxious. Grateful again for the care she showed me, I decided to re-
write the journal entry in a card and send it to my friend.

⤙ Sharing from Your Journal

A journal is a private record not meant to be shared while
we are writing in it. However, later as you reread it, there
might be things you notice about yourself or others that
can be shared as a gift or a thank-you or even an apology.
This is often best done in the context of a letter or note,
whether sent or unsent. Write that letter or note, but never
use your journal to manipulate or try to change others.

Since I am the guide for this journey, I cannot bear to end without pointing out a few things that will be helpful to keep you on the
pathway toward God. I suggest a few questions to ask as you continue along the way in your journal keeping and in your life of faith.
These are offered knowing that my own eyesight is limited; God can
always surprise us; and good advice is hard to give and harder still
to receive!

Is this a distraction, or is this the heart of the matter?

Every semester my seminary students go as a class on a retreat of solitude. While on the retreat students often need to discern whether what arises for them in the silence is a pathway toward God's presence or just something leading them away from their intention to seek God. Is this emotion or thought, this idea or impulse, a distraction or the heart of the matter? Some decide that any questions about their lives are distractions, believing that their mission is to focus solely on God. And yet what context does God have to speak into except our own lives? Another student found a soccer ball lying on the ground and longed to kick it but felt that others would think this was not "holy," seeing him having fun. Sadly, he left it sitting there, even though he realized that God himself would have caught that kick and thrown it back to him. True distractions will inevitably lead us away both from God and our true self and leave us out of sorts, confused and dissatisfied. Sometimes even our efforts to make a retreat "happen" are a distraction from what God might be doing. And sometimes what we think is a distraction is actually a word or a person (or a soccer ball) that God has placed there. The Spanish say, *"Dios te puso en mi camino"*—"God has put you in my path." Someone or something who is *Dios te puso en mi camino* is not a distraction but the heart of the matter.

Is this a critic, or is this a mentor?

The critic speaks with words of condemnation and loud judgment and hard expectations. The voice of God to those who share his love and want to live in Christ tends to be gentle and soft. A mentor sees potential, shares dreams, sometimes speaks the hard truth in love, but has earned the right to say this truth by the love that has been shared. During a visit with a close friend in California, I went on at length about all the ways that my husband and I were trying to help out my nephew Elijah, who has such serious personal and family problems. Finally my friend turned to me and gently said, "I wonder if you are

using Elijah's large problems to hide your own." These were challeng-
ing words, but they were spoken out of the love we shared, and I took
them for truth. A critic will stop you on your journey using discouragement; a mentor will nudge you forward with love.

Is this being rooted, or is this being stuck?

To be rooted is to find ourselves at home with who we are, yet always
open to the more that might be contained in the mystery of our per-
sonality or gifts or energy. We are stuck when our past failures, our
present fears, our envy of others consume us and we grow cynical and
unforgiving and closed off from the life we long for. When the corn is
planted, the farmer prays for spring rains so that the seed will germinate
and grow. But after the corn grows above the ground, the farmer prays
for the hot, dry days of summer that will cause the roots to go down
deep, reach a lower water table and cause the plant to bear the tasseled
ear of corn. When we are deeply rooted in the peace and joy and love
of Christ, it is then that we most authentically bear the fruits of the
Spirit—patience, kindness, goodness, faithfulness, gentleness and self
control. This is the true, sweet fruit of any spiritual practice, including journaling. I don't expect a cut flower to keep blooming, but when
something is rooted into the soil, I am expecting those roots to take
hold and bring forth shoots of green. Flowers may or may not appear,
but a healthy, rooted plant will continue to grow, not just inwardly but
outwardly toward the environment that it lives in. It is decorative but
also makes the atmosphere more breathable and beautiful.

Is this foolish, or is this faith's risk?

Though I am not a mountain climber, I've done my share of rock
climbing. Because one of my legs is more dependable than the other,
rock climbing might seem to be a foolish risk for a person like me. But

rock climbing always makes me face my real self—the reality of my limitations; that weaker, shorter leg; the reality of my own fears; and the reality of my determination to find a way up and over. At times rock climbing has also made me drop any pretense of control and slide down a steep side on my bottom or depend on someone else to pull me up or out. Journal teacher Luann Budd writes, "Writing honestly can lead us out to a narrow ledge, especially if we take the risk of opening our lives to the living God. . . . Taking time to journal may begin a conversation that reveals the not-so-good side. You may feel angry or afraid—sure you'll be undone. . . . Like rock climbers, when we feel most at risk our faith grows as we learn to trust Jesus to lead us to safety." Trying to do this alone, without Jesus or those who share his love and concern for you, is just plain foolishness. All of us have limitations and fears, struggles and sinful ways that require companions and guidance. But my experience as a spiritual director tells me that security is not always the most important Christian virtue. Sometimes it is neither Christian nor a virtue—it is not hiding in God but hiding out from God. There are multitudes of addictive practices and even pious attachments that can keep us from the edge where we risk opening up our lives to an awesome, dangerous, loving God.

Is this a block to my growth, or is this a challenge to grow further?
Though I am not a big football fan, I love this illustration from football—the reminder to "listen for the audibles." Even after there is a set play called, the quarterback can look out on the field, see that the set play will not work or that an opportunity has opened up, and call out an audible. Sometimes we are so set on the patterns we have in our lives that we can't hear the audibles from those around us and from God. The Gospels are full of audibles—come and see, throw your net on the other side, stretch out your hand, take up your bed

and walk, and many more. Audibles ask us to consider a new perspective, try another way, follow our creativity, be something different than we thought we could be. Blocks make us retreat further into ourselves, into the set patterns that have become not just routines but ruts. When we hear a word or have a memory that blocks us, we cannot see the way to the goal posts at all. We only feel a sense of despair, the certainty of losing. But when we listen for audibles, we suddenly see that there might be a way where we thought there was no way. Perhaps there is a way around or over or through what seemed to be an insurmountable defensive play.

Is this a detour, or is this the way home?

We are a nation in love with the superhighway—finding the fastest way from here to there. Often our goal is simply to arrive at our destination. In *Zen and the Art of Motorcycle Maintenance,* the author describes the joy that he and his son found when they discovered the back roads as a way of traveling. For them, finding that alternative route meant also finding the joy of the journey itself. Then it was no longer so much a matter of arriving at one place, but of seeing everything along the way and getting to know one another. A detour pulls us from the present with something from the past, often regret or guilt, or something from the future, often anxiety or fear. When we travel a detour, we are traveling around something that is under construction, trying to avoid the trouble that is there in plain sight. If the way means denial of the real, even real suffering, it is probably a detour. The detour might seem easier but sometimes means that we will only need to retrace our steps and travel through rather than around. Finding the long way home makes us stop and notice where we are in the present as we journey along. In the movie *Motorcycle Diaries,* young Ernesto and his friend Granado leave what seems to be a sure path to medical school and a middle-class life in Buenos Aires to take a long, circuitous journey from Argentina to Chile and Peru and Venezuela. Along the way they see everything—all the people and landscapes of South America and the mighty Amazon. Neither of them ever returns to Argentina, but their trip is still a way home for them.

At the beginning of this book, I invited all of my readers and writers on a journey with me. This journey was not to a place distant from where we are but to a place below the surface of where we are and who we are. Those of you who did the journaling exercises found that the journey was more varied than you imagined. It was all there waiting to be explored—the fear and the sin, the hurt and the loss, the cross and the empty tomb, the joy and the grace. You traveled backward to the past and looked forward into the future, then returned to stand at the crossroads of your own present moment. You began a dialogue with yourself and with God, which I hope is not ended but just begun. May the journal you have begun here in God continue to lead you toward this way of freedom and eternal life.

APPENDIX

Listening Guidelines for a Journaling Group

Listening to others read from their journaling exercise or tell about the process of writing can deepen our own understanding and practice. And the careful listening and sensitive response we give may allow the journal writer to really hear and understand what they have written. Another's willingness to read or share may help us to see something we missed when we wrote in our journal or give us the courage to read from our journal. If a journaling group chooses to write together during the group time, there is both the support of communal writing and the surprising responses that can come out of journaling in the present moment. Creating an inviting and safe place for journaling is an essential requirement for a supportive and nurturing journaling group. The guidelines that follow are designed to create that safe environment through mutual agreement about how the group members will both share and listen. It is helpful to read these aloud at the beginning and get the consent of the group as a whole. This allows the group members to be accountable and care for one another and offer gentle reminders about how they already agreed to honor one another in their listening and sharing, their writing and reading.

SHARING FROM YOUR JOURNAL
OR YOUR WRITING PROCESS

1. Share what is appropriate for you. You may always choose to talk about the process of journaling or about the experience of writing itself, rather than reading directly from your journal. This protects the privacy of each person's journal. Include readings and reflections that are illuminating but do not expose you in any way that makes you feel uncomfortable.

2. Share what seems to be the "heart of the matter" for you. The "heart of the matter" is the place where you felt the most energy, or seemed to be most alive and connected with who you truly are or what you want to say. It might be the place where you saw something new; a familiar place you revisited, almost as if seeing it for the first time; or a place where you feel puzzled and stuck but have a sense that there is more going on there. This is not necessarily a place of misery or joy—it is a place of discovery.

3. Do not judge, criticize or apologize for your writing or your writing experience. Some of us want to apologize as we speak, or explain or interpret what we have written for others. Please don't. Let your words speak for themselves. They don't need you to defend them or refute them.

RESPONDING TO OTHERS
IN THE JOURNALING GROUP

1. Respect the confidentiality of others. Always remember that anything shared in a journaling group cannot be shared outside of the group, unless permission is received. This is true for positive reflections as well as hard or difficult ones.

2. *Let your response show that you are hearing what seems to be the heart of what the other person is saying.* Ask yourself, *in what has been shared, what do I hear, what do I see, what moves me?* Try to respond with your whole self—feelings, intuition, intellect, imagination.

3. *Share a response that will deepen or enhance the reflection.* Ask yourself, *is my response going to help the person notice something about the experience itself or understand it on a deeper level? Or is this just personal curiousity?*

4. *Speak for yourself only, and share your own experiences without generalizations.* Our sharing should be authentic and not second-hand. Share your own story in response with care that it doesn't diminish or tear down someone else's experience.

5. *Do not judge, criticize or challenge what someone says.* In order to have the safest possible environment in which people can explore their deepest thoughts and feelings without fear of being criticized, we need to allow for different points of view. Rather than say, "I disagree," you might want to offer something from your own experience with an alternative viewpoint.

6. *Do not give advice or try to "fix" someone's problem or viewpoint.* Journaling together is a sharing of presence and not problem solving. Sometimes we are uncomfortable letting people remain in a difficult place. Commit to praying for one another, and leave each other in the care of the Almighty.

7. *One final word: hold your desires and opinions—even your convictions—lightly.* No person or group can comprehend God. No matter how intelligent and holy we are, our grasp of reality is always limited. We need not discard our convictions. But it behooves us to hold them lightly, as if they were resting on our open hands. In this way we invite God to take them from us to refine them, strengthen them or perhaps replace them.

NOTES

Chapter 1: Starting Out

page 13   O God! Dig into my life: Calvin Seerveld, trans., *Voicing God's Psalms* (Grand Rapids: Eerdmans, 2005), p. 81.

page 20   "God is already present": Gary Moon, "Experiencing the Presence of God: A Conversation with James Finley," in *Conversations* 4, no. 2 (fall 2006): 21.

Chapter 2: Beginning Again

page 21   Trosly, France: Henri Nouwen, *The Road to Daybreak* (New York: Doubleday, 1988), p. 7.

page 22   Friday, December 13: Ibid., pp. 94-95.

page 25   October 23: Anne Lamott, *Operating Instructions: A Journal of My Son's First Year* (New York: Anchor Books, 1993), p. 82.

page 26   November 30: Ibid., p. 112.

page 26   March 20: Ibid., p. 176.

page 27   June 16: Ibid., p. 221.

page 28   "There is no deep knowledge": John Calvin, *Institutes of the Christian Religion,* quoted in David G. Benner, *The Gift of Being Yourself: The Sacred Call to Self-Discovery* (Downers Grove, Ill.: InterVarsity Press, 2004), p. 20.

page 28   "clear, easy brightness": Philip Moulton, ed., *The Journal and Major Essays of John Woolman* (New York: Oxford University Press, 1971), p. 58.

Chapter 3: Looking Intently

page 33   it is this interior movement: Alexandra Johnson, *Leaving a Trace* (Boston: Little, Brown, 2001), p. 30.

page 35   "long, loving look": Walter J. Burghardt, "Contemplation: A Long Loving Look at the Real" *Church* 5, no. 4 (winter 1989): 14-18.

Chapter 4: Claiming Significance

page 44   Reflections on Your Name: Adapted from G. Lynn Nelson, *Writing and Being: Embracing Your Life Through Creative Journaling* (Maui, Hawaii: Inner Ocean Publishing, 2004), p. 45.

page 45   "God is known": Walter Brueggemann, *Genesis,* Interpretation: A Biblical Commentary for Preaching and Teaching (Atlanta: John Knox Press, 1980), p. 32.

page 45   "Nothing but the raw power": Naomi Rosenblatt and Joshua Horvitz, *Wrestling with Angels* (New York: Delta, 1995), p. 21.

Chapter 5: Naming the Landscape

page 53   "The first and greatest fear": Pat Schneider, *Writing Alone and with Others* (Oxford: Oxford University Press, 2003), p. 3

page 54   "Where there is fear": Ibid., p. 4.

page 54   most frequent command: N. T. Wright, *Following Jesus: Biblical Reflections on Discipleship* (Grand Rapids: Eerdmans, 1994), p. 66.

page 55   "I found myself": Leonard Kriegel, *Falling into Life: Essays* (San Francisco: North Point Press, 1991), p. 13.

page 58   Journaling Focus: Changes: Adapted from Virginia Hearn, *Just As I Am: Journal-Keeping for Spiritual Growth* (Grand Rapids: Revell, 1994), p. 54.

Chapter 6: Listening Beyond Words

page 63   "The body doesn't lie": Tristine Rainer, *Your Life as Story: Writing* the *New Autobiography* (New York: G. P. Putnam's Sons, 1997), p. 202.

page 66   Stephanie Paulsell tells: Stephanie Paulsell, "Honoring the Body," in *Practicing Our Faith: A Way of Life for a Searching People*, ed. Dorothy Bass (New York: Jossey-Bass, 2002), p. 19.

page 70   Loving Word of God: Janet Morley, *All Desires Known* (Harrisburg, Penn.: Morehouse, 1992), p. 87.

Chapter 7: Looking Backward

page 72   "each of us must": Patricia Hampl, *I Could Tell You Stories: Sojourns in the Land of Memory* (New York: W. W. Norton, 1999), p. 32.

page 75   "Like the Israelites": Wilkie Au, *The Enduring Heart: Spirituality for the Long Haul* (New York: Paulist Press, 2000), p. 69.

page 75   My thoughtful friend: Thanks to Laryssa Sadoway for this insight.

page 76   "Full of surprises": Alexandra Johnson, *Leaving a Trace: On Keeping a Journal* (Boston: Little, Brown, 2001), p. 116.

page 79   "sifting through": Suzanne Farnham, ed., *Listening Hearts: Discerning Call in Community* (Harrisburg, Penn.: Morehouse, 1991), p. 23.

page 80   "come to the place": Dennis Covington, *Salvation on Sand Mountain: Snake Handling and Redemption in Southern Appalachia* (Reading, Mass.: Addison-Wesley, 1995).

page 80   The heart's *metanoia*: Scott Cairns, "Adventures in New Testament Greek: Metanoia," in *Philokalia: New and Selected Poems* (Lincoln, Nebr.: Zoo Press, 2002), p. 15.

Chapter 8: Looking Forward

page 83   Make a List: Ron Klug, *How to Keep a Spiritual Journal*, rev. ed. (Minneapolis: Augsburg Press, 2002), p. 89.

page 85   Storyteller Megan McKenna: Megan McKenna, *Parables: The Arrows of God* (Maryknoll, N.Y.: Orbis, 1994), pp. 28-29.

page 87   Waiting and Hoping: Jan Johnson, "Contemplation: No Better
            Place to Be Than with God," *Conversations* 4, no. 2 (2006).
page 90   What Jesus did: Krista Tippett, *Speaking of Faith* (New York:
            Viking, 2007), p. 12.

Chapter 9: Reorienting in the Present

page 93   My Personal Compass: Adapted from Wilkie Au, *The Enduring
            Heart: Spirituality for the Long Haul* (New York: Paulist Press,
            2001), pp. 49-50.
page 100   "What we need": Ronald Rolheiser, *The Shattered Lantern: Redis-
            covering a Felt Presence of God* (New York: Crossroads Publishing,
            2001), p. 186.
page 101   "Our 'behavior'": Donald Miller, *Blue Like Jazz* (Nashville:
            Thomas Nelson, 2003), p. 86.

Chapter 10: Talking Back

page 105   "As strange as it may sound": Ruth Haley Barton, *Invitation to
            Solitude and Silence* (Downers Grove, Ill.: InterVarsity Press,
            2004), p. 30.
page 106   "Underlying these": Ira Progroff, *At a Journal Workshop: The Basic
            Text and Guide for Using the Intensive Journal* (New York: Dialogue
            House Library, 1975), p. 159.

Chapter 11: Embracing the Cross

page 115   Jesus at his crucifixion: Walter Wink, *Engaging the Powers: Dis-
            cernment and Resistance in a World of Domination* (Minneapolis:
            Fortress, 1992), p. 141.
page 116   "I write": Kate Newton, "No Easy Answers," unpublished
            essay.
page 118   helpful resource: Megan McKenna, *The New Stations of the Cross:
            The Way of the Cross According to Scripture* (New York: Image
            Books, 2003).

page 119   I never suspected: Ronald Rolheiser, "Mary Magdala's Easter
                Prayer," in *Forgotten Among the Lilies* (New York: Doubleday,
                2005), p. 176.
page 122   "worshiping Jesus' journey": Richard Rohr, *Everything Belongs: The
                Gift of Contemplative Prayer* (New York: Crossroads, 2003), p. 20.

Chapter 12: Discovering Life

page 124   "I don't even believe in God": Mary Karr, *Sinners Welcome* (New
                York: HarperCollins, 2006), p. 77.
page 124   "I started to follow": Ibid., p. 83.
page 125   Heart Wounds and Scars: Adapted from G. Lynn Nelson,
                Writing and Being: Embracing Your Life Through Creative Journaling
                (Maui, Hawaii: Inner Ocean Publishing, 2004), p. 118.
page 126   "You must be convinced of this": Brennan Manning, *The Raga-
                muffin Gospel* (Portland, Ore.: Multnomah, 1990), p. 86.
page 127   This idea that God: Melanie Jansen, *From the Darkest Night: Med-
                itations for Abuse Survivors* (Grand Rapids: Faith Alive Christian
                Resources, 2001), p. 20.
page 129   Being abused: Ibid., p. 45.
page 129   "Perhaps, I reasoned": Ibid., p. 46.
page 130   Putting my hope: Ibid., p. 69.
page 132   "Look! It is winter": Robert Collen, "Le Cri de Merlin," in
                Burning World: Poems (Athol, Mass.: Haleys, 1997), p. 47.

Chapter 13: Seeing the Holy in the Ordinary

page 137   "Earth's crammed with heaven": Elizabeth Barrett Browning,
                Aurora Leigh: A Poem in Nine Books, bk. 7, ed. Margaret Reynolds
                (Athens: Ohio University Press, 1992), lines 821-24, p. 487.
page 138   "What a surprise": John Shea, *The Legend of the Bells and Other
                Tales: Stories of the Human Spirit* (Chicago: ACTA Publications,
                1996), pp. 7-8.
page 140   "The world is charged": Gerard Manley Hopkins, "God's Gran-
                deur," in *The Poems of Gerard Manley Hopkins,* 4th ed., ed. W. H.

Gardner and N. H. Mackenzie (Oxford: Oxford University Press, 1984), p. 66.

Chapter 14: Facing Resistance

page 144 But one Haggadah: Steve Waldman, "The Waldman Family Haggadah," (2006), posted on Beliefnet.com <http://www.beliefnet.com/story/165/story_16522.html>.

page 146 Keeping a journal: Thomas Merton, *Sign of Jonas* (Garden City, N.Y.: Doubleday, 1956), p. 201.

page 146 Bringing It Forward: Ron Klug, *How to Keep a Spiritual Journal* (Minneapolis: Augsburg, 2002), p. 125.

page 150 "Writing honestly": Luann Budd, *Journal Keeping: Writing for Spritual Growth* (Downers Grove, Ill.: InterVarsity Press, 2002), p. 170.

page 151 "listen for the audibles": Wilkie Au and Noreen Cannon Au, *The Discerning Heart: Exploring the Christian Path* (New York: Paulist Press, 2006), p. 23.

Appendix: Listening Guidelines for a Journaling Group

page 153 The guidelines that follow. Adapted from Suzanne G. Farnham, Stephanie A. Hull and R. Taylor McLean, *Grounded in God. Listening Hearts Discernment for Group Deliberations* (Harrisburg, Penn.: Morehouse, 1999), pp. 58-61.

*f*ormatio
TRADITION. EXPERIENCE.
TRANSFORMATION

Formatio books from InterVarsity Press follow the rich tradition of the church in the journey of spiritual formation. These books are not merely about being informed, but about being transformed by Christ and conformed to his image. Formatio stands in InterVarsity Press's evangelical publishing tradition by integrating God's Word with spiritual practice and by prompting readers to move from inward change to outward witness. InterVarsity Press uses the chambered nautilus for Formatio, a symbol of spiritual formation because of its continual spiral journey outward as it moves from its center. We believe that each of us is made with a deep desire to be in God's presence. Formatio books help us to fulfill our deepest desires and to become our true selves in light of God's grace.